The Employee Satisfaction
REVOLUTION

Understanding and Unleashing
the Power of a Satisfied Workforce

BY DR. PATRICIA BUHLER AND JASON SCOTT

PRESTWICK HOUSE, INC.

"Everything for the English Classroom!"

P.O. BOX 658 CLAYTON, DELAWARE 19938

Writers

Dr. Patricia Buhler

Jason Scott

Editors

Magedah Shabo

Paul Moliken

Cover and Text Design

Larry Knox

Production

Jeremy Clark

PRESTWICK HOUSE, INC.

"Everything for the English Classroom!"

ISBN: 978-1-60843-998-0

Reorder No. 305036

The Employee Satisfaction
REVOLUTION

Understanding and Unleashing
the Power of a Satisfied Workforce

Table of Contents

Preface

MANY COMPANIES PAY LIP SERVICE to the ideal of having satisfied employees. But when these organizations neglect to build their cultures around that goal, their claims are hollow at best and destructive at worst. That's why in this book, we've set out to demonstrate how a company can change "employee satisfaction" from a mere slogan into a reality. *The Employee Satisfaction Revolution* combines the academic insights of Dr. Patricia Buhler with the real-life experiences of Jason Scott, CEO of Prestwick House, Inc.—a Delaware publishing company that has enjoyed tremendous growth largely because of its emphasis on employee satisfaction.

This book takes a new approach to strategic employee management that will be valuable to business owners, managers, human resource professionals, and students alike. ✿

Authors

Pat Buhler has been a professor of management at Goldey-Beacom College in Wilmington, Delaware, since 1989. She specializes in management, human resource management, and strategy courses in both the graduate and undergraduate programs. She holds a doctorate in business administration and an MBA.

Pat has authored two books, *Teach Yourself Management Skills in 24 Hours* and *Human Resources Management: All the Information You Need to Manage Your Staff and Meet Your Business Objectives*, as well as over 150 published articles. She is the owner of Buhler Business Consultants, a firm that has operated for over 20 years, specializing in human capital solutions for businesses.

Jason Scott has worked for Prestwick House since 1997, initially as the Operations Manager and currently as CEO. Prior to that, he worked for the National Endowment for the Arts in Washington, D.C. During his tenure at Prestwick House, the educational publishing company has grown from just over $1 million in annual revenue to over $8 million in revenue. Having  earned his MBA from Goldey-Beacom College in 2000, Jason implemented an ongoing strategic planning program that established company-wide goals and operational benchmarks. Among these was the goal of making Prestwick House the best company to work for in Delaware. Jason credits the organization's work towards that goal with its 2008 recognition as the fourth-best publishing company in the country to work for by *Book Business Magazine*.

INTRODUCTION

DR. PATRICIA BUHLER

THIS BOOK IS A COLLABORATIVE EFFORT of a somewhat unique nature. Starting out as a regular relationship between professor and student, my friendship with Jason has evolved to the point where our roles have, in a sense, begun to reverse, and I have found that I have much to learn from him. I am pleased to have been able to collaborate with him on this project.

In a field of delightful, achievement-oriented MBA students, Jason stood out from the crowd. Jason eloquently articulated a philosophy I had seldom heard: he didn't care as much about the grade he received as he cared about learning something that he could use in his business. He proved to be an excellent student, constantly focusing on the application of the concepts presented. And he returned to his business to use these ideas and grow a successful enterprise. Through the years since his graduation, Jason has stayed in touch, sending updates and thanks to all the faculty members. Eventually, he agreed to teach some adjunct courses, and, in fulfillment of his need to "give back," he became a regular guest lecturer in our strategic management course. As a living illustration of the importance of the course and the program, he offered concrete examples of how he used the material he had learned at Goldey-Beacom in his own business. Jason has helped me to reinforce the connection between the classroom concepts of organizational dynamics and the real world in immeasurable ways.

When he approached me about co-authoring a book, I jumped at the opportunity—only to realize that the real message to be communicated was his. My contribution to the project was merely to provide an explanation of why his ideas are so important. He has taken the tools we discussed in class and successfully implemented them in his organization to create the type of company where people want to come to work, where they are valued, and where they are provided the opportunity to prosper personally and professionally. Jason takes the textbook concepts of human resource management and clearly demonstrates that they are doable. And what's more, all organizations can achieve this kind of success—if they follow his advice.

Jason has the real story of how to create a revolution in your own business. I will just share insights from the research that demonstrate why a satisfied workforce is so important.

JASON SCOTT

WHEN I CAME TO WORK WITH MY FATHER, Jim, in his educational publishing business, the company was earning just under $1 million per year. He had three employees: my mother and two non-family members. Jim started the business in 1980, but he had basically been running it like a hobby for the first fifteen years of its life. He hadn't put real management processes in place and was, like a lot of small business owners, operating on a crisis-to-crisis basis.

However, he knew he had a good product and wanted to see if the business could grow beyond being a successful start-up. He also knew that his aversion to managing people was a serious crisis just waiting to happen. For all Jim's entrepreneurial virtues, he was a lousy manager. He only gave feedback when something was going wrong, and then only after it had been a problem for a long while. He would let problems go uncorrected in the hope that they would somehow disappear; but, while the problems failed to go away, they continued to eat away at him. After an issue had been gnawing at him for a while, he would suddenly lose his temper without any warning. The low man on the company's four-person totem pole would quit regularly after one of these outbursts, only to return to work the following day.

It would be fair to call my father's management style "old school." Like others of his generation, he had an attitude that said to employees, "Do what I say because I'm smarter than you." If that didn't work, Plan B was, "Do what I say because I'm the one cutting the checks." And when that failed, "If you don't like it, quit!" From his perspective, these phrases contained all that anyone needed to know about human resource management.

To his credit, though, Jim was aware of his strengths and weaknesses, and he knew that to grow the business beyond the cottage-industry phase, he would need someone with a more developed sense of human resource management. When I joined the company, he was glad to make dealing with people one of my responsibilities.

Having worked in schools his whole career, Jim was familiar with dysfunctional workplaces. In fact, we had both worked in places that made you want to throw up at the thought of Monday morning. We had a lot of common ground when it came to figuring out what kind of company we wanted Prestwick House to become as it grew; most importantly, we didn't want Prestwick House to become a place where employees started feeling nauseated when Sunday night came around.

One of my first jobs was at a large American auto company's parts and warehouse/distribution center, in which everyone was counting down the days until retirement. And I don't mean, "I have six months to go"—it was more like, "I can't wait for the next 13 years to be over so I can retire."

As someone just finishing college, to be in a workplace where people hated their jobs—and were resigned to hating their jobs—was a startling experience for me. I saw this apathy demonstrated one day when an expensive brake part fell off a pallet that was being sent to dealers. There had been a recall, so keeping track of each part and knowing where it fit was important. Finding an orphaned part near the loading dock, I asked one of the longer-term employees where I could find the printout that would tell me where this part belonged. He held out his hand in a gesture I understood to mean that he wanted to look at the part. When I handed him the box, he took the expensive part, still in pristine condition, and launched it 50 feet towards an open dumpster, where it slammed in like the buzzer-beating three-point shot in a college basketball game.

"Nobody gives a damn about that part," he said matter-of-factly to me as he walked away. That was when it dawned on me why cars are so expensive. That was also when I realized that most people viewed their jobs as something not to enjoy, but to endure.

When I went to work with my father, years later, we both knew one thing about the company we wanted to build. We didn't want it to be the kind of workplace that people merely endured. We agreed that whatever else it became, Prestwick House would always be a pleasant place to work.

Of course, knowing what you want to do and doing it are two different things. So, before I say anything else about how we achieved our goals, I need to acknowledge Goldey-Beacom College.

When I joined my father, we didn't have much formal business knowledge between us. He had a lot of product knowledge from his years in the classroom, and he also had a great marketer's sense of what customers wanted and how they should be approached. But beyond that, our collective business knowledge was lacking. So, I went to get my master's degree from Goldey-Beacom College. That was a true turning point for the business because it made me begin thinking strategically.

From Pat Buhler and other tremendous faculty members at Goldey-Beacom, I learned to align the goals of marketing, finance, operations, and human resources. The Goldey-Beacom master's program emphasized strategic thinking, and its curriculum underscored the fact that when a company's diverse goals are all aligned, great things can happen. Understanding that many businesses allow departments to compete with each other for scarce resources and enter into counterproductive infighting, the Goldey-Beacom curriculum instead stressed strategic thinking.

Being in grad school was an exciting time for me because everything that I learned at Goldey-Beacom was directly applicable to this new business I was building with my father. I remember coming home from class and being able to immediately see how I could implement the techniques I had just learned. And I got to see the impact of these changes directly. I witnessed how the theories on the page were actually working in real life. On a daily basis, I could see that it was true that if you aligned goals across departments, those goals would have a greater impact and that if you viewed HR management not as an expense, but as an investment in the company, it would be an investment well made.

So, for me, the point of this book is to share some of the techniques we've put in place over the years and to help managers and business owners improve their companies by focusing on employee satisfaction. My contribution to this book is the anecdotal, case-study side.

I like to set objectives high, while finding fulfillment in small achievements along the way. My big goal for this book is to awaken American businesses to the power of a satisfied employee base and to launch a major change in the way American businesses are run. That is not a modest goal, but I think it is doable. The small, "along the way" goal is to give everyone who reads this book some practical tools for improving employee morale.

I'm convinced that if you try focusing your organization on employee satisfaction, even just a little bit, you'll begin to see results in no time. ✹

Employee Satisfaction: A Potential Source of Competitive Advantage

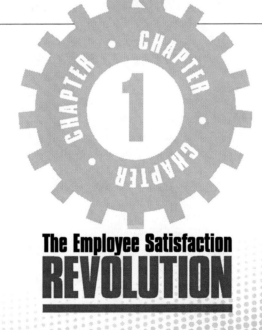

The Employee Satisfaction
REVOLUTION

Employee Satisfaction: A Potential Source of Competitive Advantage

"The people in the company make the organization what it is. They are the ones creating the assets of the organization."

Lior Arussy[1]

IT IS DISTURBING TO READ in the research reported from studies of American businesses that there has been a substantial decline in overall job satisfaction in recent decades. In the United States, there is a great deal of employee dissatisfaction. Nearly 25 percent of the workforce in America is said to be "simply showing up to collect a paycheck."[2] In the 1990s, Judith Bardwick coined the phrase "face time" to describe this phenomenon, in which workers behave as if they are entitled to collect a regular paycheck for merely showing up to work[3]. Unfortunately, it would appear that this approach is still thriving in the twenty-first century. Most American workers are "retired on the job"—physically present, but mentally absent.

In fact, job satisfaction seems to be at an all-time low. Recent studies describe nearly 40% of American workers as "disconnected" from their employers[4]. Reports show that only 20 percent of workers surveyed feel passionate about their jobs[5], and nearly one-third of workers think they have reached a career plateau[6]. It should come as no surprise, then, that approximately 66 percent of workers are not motivated to contribute to their organization's goals[7]. These statistics should serve as a warning for all businesses—and as a challenge. While employee dissatisfaction predicts trouble for organizations that choose to do nothing, it also provides an opportunity for growth. It means that companies are leaving potential for improved company productivity untapped. While failure to address employee satisfaction can mean poor performance, the good news is that addressing employee satisfaction can provide the source of a competitive advantage for those organizations that choose to proactively meet the challenge.

The competitive landscape of business has created a situation in which every company wages a war each day for its basic survival. Each organization, however, has an incredible source of power in its employees. The purpose of this book is to help organizations understand how this power can be unleashed. With improved employee satisfaction, companies can have the opportunity to experience a wealth of benefits, including lower turnover, higher productivity levels, improved customer satisfaction, higher profit levels, and even awards and accolades.

The approach to employee satisfaction suggested in this book is indeed radical. In a highly competitive business landscape, organizations don't have the luxury of slowly letting this concept evolve. The changes required today call for revolution, not evolution, and each organization must address how it will begin its own employee satisfaction revolution.

The Question of Causality

Employee satisfaction can drive business outcomes and can be the foundation and the source of a firm's competitive advantage. But, simply put, employee satisfaction may be one of the most underutilized resources in many organizations. Higher levels of employee satisfaction can provide a firm with a competitive edge in hiring and retaining employees. As the war for talent is waged, this becomes even more critical.

While the importance of employee satisfaction is generally accepted by most astute organizations, researchers have debated the issue of causality. Though correlation does not prove causation, there is research that supports the intuitive notion that highly satisfied employees will work harder, better understand how they can contribute to their company's bottom line, and, thereby, cause the company to perform better in a number of areas. Those employees who are highly satisfied will be better able, and more likely, to align their own talents and abilities with the mission and objectives of the organization. Satisfied employees better understand how to contribute to the organization's success.

The business case for employee satisfaction has been well document-ed. In *The Loyalty Effect*, Fred Reichheld suggests that there are clear links between customer satisfaction, employee satisfaction, and financial perfor-mance[8]. These conclusions are also echoed by Jim Heskett, Earl Sasser, and Len Schlesinger in *The Service Profit Chain*. They also propose that employee satisfaction leads to greater perceived product value, which, in turn, leads to customer satisfaction and, ultimately, to organizational profits[9].

High levels of employee satisfaction have been positively correlated with customer loyalty and company profitability in other studies as well. A 2001 *Personnel Psychology* study explored the causation relationship, concluding not only that the satisfaction levels of employees can predict the profitability of a firm, but also that there is a strong positive correlation between employee satisfaction and customer satisfaction[10]. Similarly, a study by Watson Wyatt Worldwide finds that human resource practices can improve financial perfor-mance[11], and a report by Price Waterhouse Coopers suggests that employee satisfaction impacts long-term shareholder returns[12].

Creating and maintaining high levels of employee satisfaction should not be viewed as an addendum, but, instead, as an essential part of a company's strategy. As part of an integrated approach, the benefits of boosting employee morale can be substantial. What's more, a failure to address employee sat-isfaction comes with a high price tag. The Gallop organization has reported that employees who are actively disengaged have cost American businesses over $300 billion in lost productivity[13]. At extreme levels of dissatisfaction, disengaged employees may purposely sabotage an organization, which can lead to disastrous consequences.

This is not to suggest that companies with low levels of employee satisfac-tion cannot experience high performance levels, but success is certainly is not as likely for such organizations. In a highly competitive business landscape, companies have even less room to allow dissatisfaction to fester. Some com-panies may succeed financially in spite of themselves, as their managers rule by fear and intimidation, with no regard for the satisfaction of their employ-ees. The message from this data is hopeful, though—there is vast opportu-nity for financial growth if such organizations will begin to pay attention to employee satisfaction.

Towards a New Understanding of Job Satisfaction

In today's business environment, it would behoove managers to define job satisfaction more broadly than has been the traditional approach. The expanded definition should include a sense of fulfillment, empowerment, and engagement. The result of a broader approach, according to Michael Leimbach is "a powerful tool for creating a high-performance, high-fulfillment work environment."[14]

This expanded definition of job satisfaction addresses whether employees are fulfilled at work, whether they have positive relationships with their coworkers, and whether they trust their leaders. This moves beyond the traditional definition of job satisfaction, which considered only the individual. This broader concept of fulfillment also takes into account the views of coworkers—who can definitely influence any employee's perception of a job and the level of satisfaction he or she is likely to experience. It is indeed a reciprocal relationship. Interestingly enough, open communication works to the advantage of those organizations with highly satisfied employees, since they share their positive feelings with others. The ultimate impact is higher organizational performance.

Much of the research generally demonstrates correlation rather than causation—and Prestwick House presents a great case for understanding employee satisfaction and using that knowledge to create a sustainable competitive advantage, and to outperform the competition. ✿

The Prestwick House Approach to Employee Satisfaction

The Employee Satisfaction
REVOLUTION

THE PRESTWICK HOUSE APPROACH TO EMPLOYEE SATISFACTION

"The things I like most about my job at Prestwick House are the overall atmosphere, the sense of teamwork and pride in what we are doing, and the fact that once my unique skills became apparent, they were immediately put to good use."

PRESTWICK HOUSE EMPLOYEE

The Prestwick House Approach

THE PURSUIT OF EMPLOYEE SATISFACTION at Prestwick House does not mean that everyone is happy all the time. The fact that we're working towards creating a culture of contented employees does not mean that the company is engaged in babying everyone and jumping through hoops to ameliorate every gripe and grievance that arises. But what it does mean is that early on, we made a deliberate choice to focus on overall employee satisfaction as a way to grow the company. (Indeed, as the pragmatic entrepreneur reading this book should be relieved to learn, there is a financial consideration at the heart of what sounds a lot like touchy-feely HR talk.)

Knowing that many people dread going to work, we wanted to build a company culture at Prestwick House that people would enjoy. Even when the company was tiny, we set the absurd goal of becoming "widely recognized as the best place to work in Delaware," and that goal has guided a lot of our decisions over the years. Along the way, we discovered that there were solid, economic reasons to make sure people liked working here.

Obviously, as Prestwick House aspired to be "the best place to work," we made a deliberate choice to give our staff ample pay and benefits. We found that this was an area in which we could gain an advantage that would help us compete with larger, better established publishing companies.

Whereas other companies might have decided to invest in their IT infrastructure over the next ten years, we at Prestwick House decided that we were going to invest in employee satisfaction. It's an investment that continues to pay off extremely well. But it takes a lot more to build a satisfied team than simply money. The company is invested in its people as part of our corporate mission, and Prestwick House has found that our workers' happiness has as much to do with creating norms of behavior that work for everyone as it does with building a decent benefits package.

An essential step in creating those cultural norms that lead to employee satisfaction is to give everyone a clear sense of our broad strategic goals and the tools needed to achieve those goals. We think of it as a high-flexibility, high-accountability approach, and our goal in this is to allow everyone to be as self-managed as possible. Putting this philosophy into practice means that we are always on guard against policies that reduce flexibility, while we are also constantly trying to formulate goals and procedures that increase accountability.

Prestwick House Flexibility & Accountability

High

Artist Commune — PH

FLEXIBILITY

DMV — Factory

Low — High

ACCOUNTABILITY

Flexibility and accountability are critical to the employee-centric culture, and the growth of policies and practices at Prestwick House was organic in nature. That is, policies were not filtered through the question of whether any given change would make employees more satisfied. Instead, they were examined through the questions, "Does this make sense?" and, "Does this help our customers?"

The policies and practices that survive are those that underscore our desire to ensure that people find their work satisfying and that they are getting appropriate positive and negative feedback. Ultimately, the Prestwick House system is designed to encourage all employees to feel that they are not simply doing a job, but that they are also helping to build a company—and most people find that immensely rewarding. ✿

An Overview of the Employee Satisfaction Revolution Model

The Employee Satisfaction
REVOLUTION

- Satisfied Customers
- Low Turnover
- High Productivity
- Recruitment Advantage
- Financial Success

Organizational Culture

Bottom Line

Employee Statisfaction

Leadership
- Strategic Planning
- Ethics
- Authentic Leadership
- Transparency

Organizational Culture
- Trust
- Communication
- Empowerment
- Fun

HR Strategies
- Work/Life Balance
- Recruitment
- Employee Motivation
- Training & Development
- Performance Appraisals

EMPLOYEE SATISFACTION REVOLUTION

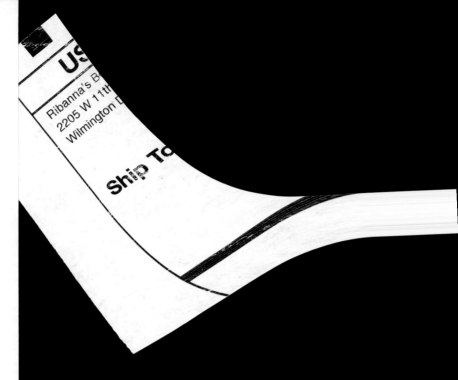

US

Ribanna's B
2205 W 11th
Wilmington D

Ship To

"...there is a significant and meaningful relationship be-
tween business performance and fulfillment...organizations,
regardless of industry, could improve organizational per-
formance by improving fulfillment among employees."
MICHAEL LEIMBACH[1]

THE MODEL PRESENTED HERE helps to describe the various "levers" that can be used to bring about employee satisfaction (which, in turn, positively impacts the organization's bottom line). These elements include organizational culture, leadership, and HR strategies. Each of these may be considered a lever by which employee satisfaction can be increased. There are specific recommendations and best practices that enable effective leveraging of these elements in creating and maintaining a satisfied workforce. Readers are encouraged, though, to think broadly and customize these concepts to best fit their own organizational needs and opportunities. Best practices of other organizations can provide the guidelines, but from there, each organization must come up with its own unique approach.

Companies have used a number of models in assessing the links between employee satisfaction and various measures of company performance.

For example, Sears used the model from the *The Service Profit Chain*[2] to determine that an increase of five percent in employee satisfaction resulted in an increase of 1.3 percent in customer satisfaction; this change yielded an increase of 0.5 percent in revenue growth. Amazingly, Sears later reported that 60 to 80 percent of their customer satisfaction was attributable to employee satisfaction[3].

PNC Bank has reported an impressive 84 percent correlation between customer satisfaction and employee satisfaction[4]. In another remarkable story, Nortel found that its customer satisfaction rates improved drastically after the company resolved problems that had hindered its employee satisfaction levels. The firm confidently concluded that improved employee satisfaction can lead to greater customer satisfaction and, in turn, to improved financial results[5].

Sun Microsystems has its own unique system for measuring employee satisfaction against customer satisfaction. The company conducts monthly polls to determine employee satisfaction levels and subsequently calculates an "employee quality index," which is then compared to figures related to customer loyalty[6].

ACNielsen follows a similar approach to measuring their employees' satisfaction. They have found that financial performance improves shortly after employee satisfaction levels improve. Accordingly, ACNielsen has aligned their managers' bonuses with business unit scores for employee satisfaction[7].

The innovative agricultural firm Monsanto surveyed the work/life balance of their employees and found that customer satisfaction could be predicted by two key measures—one of which was the work/life balance of Monsanto employees[8].

As for methods of measuring changes in employee turnover rates, we can look to Just Born, a candy company based in Pennsylvania, and Cisco System for models. Just Born reports an almost 50 percent reduction in turnover (reduced to only 2%) accompanying the introduction of an "employee-focused culture."[9]

The key to the three levers of the employee satisfaction model is using them together—when combined, they have a greater impact than they would individually. It's almost counterproductive to discuss the three levers in separate chapters since it is the *interaction* of the culture, the leadership, and the HR strategies that creates an employee satisfaction revolution.

The culture of an organization reflects the DNA of the company, tells people "how we do things around here," and explains what kinds of behaviors are valued. Employee satisfaction levels tend to be higher in employee-centric cultures that are characterized by trust, transparency, open communication, and innovation.

The leadership of a company plays a major role in the employee satisfaction revolution; it won't just happen by itself. A concerted effort to focus on the right elements within the organization can positively affect employee

ance. Organizations focused on employee satisfaction pay particular attention to hiring the right individuals for the job, providing them with opportunities to develop, and measuring their performance in terms of achieving corporate objectives.

Those elements that comprise the larger corporate objectives—or the "bottom line"—are depicted in the ES model and are discussed in Chapter 8. It's important to track these visible results that demonstrate the return on your investment in your employees.

But for now, let's talk about the first step to creating your own ES Revolution—establishing the ideal organizational culture. ✪

The Employee Satisfaction
REVOLUTION

- Satisfied Customers
- Low Turnover
- High Productivity
- Recruitment Advantage
- Financial Success

Bottom Line

Organizational Culture

Employee Statisfaction

Leadership
- Strategic Planning
- Ethics
- Authentic Leadership
- Transparency

Organizational Culture
- Trust
- Communication
- Empowerment
- Fun

HR Strategies
- Work/Life Balance
- Recruitment
- Employee Motivation
- Training & Development
- Performance Appraisals

"Culture is an abstraction, yet the forces that are created in social and organizational situations that derive from culture are powerful."

EDGAR H. SCHEIN[1]

AS STATED EARLIER, culture might be considered the DNA of an organization. It directs and informs the behavior of a diverse group of individuals as they function, like the diverse cells of the body, in separate, but interrelated roles. Culture can even be the source of an organization's competitive advantage.

Building and maintaining a productive corporate culture is one of a manager's most significant responsibilities. The development of corporate culture cannot be left to chance, but must, rather, be consciously decided. The founders of the organization usually transfer their own personal values to the company. A compelling example is provided by the late Sam Walton, whose personal beliefs naturally evolved into the corporate values embraced by Wal-Mart. His competitiveness was demonstrated in the firm's corporate philosophy, with its focus on excellence. His religious, small-town upbringing translated into an emphasis on respect for the individual—whether employee or customer.

A similar example can be found in Delaware, where the corporate culture of the former MBNA was well understood and well publicized in the community. The management of MBNA placed a high value on customer service, and the company's service motto was even written across every doorway in each of their office buildings. Every manager from all company functional areas had to spend two to four hours each month on the phones with customers, which reinforced MBNA's emphasis on customer service. This strong culture of respect for customers was reinforced in the policies and processes of the organization.

It's not enough to say it or write it—a company must also practice its values if it wants them to be reflected in the actual corporate culture. Some organizations publish written values statements to a great deal of fanfare, with employees throughout the organization briefly celebrating what the company believes in, but ultimately having little more than a glossy wallet card to remind them of their organization's supposed values.

While this approach can certainly work, success requires that the focus be on the values themselves, instead of merely their declaration. Ideally, an organization will build a strong culture around the values of its founder and the rites of the organization, and employees should be regularly be reminded of what the organization stands for and how people are expected to behave. These values serve to guide decision making and clearly communicate what people are expected to do. And despite conventional practice, these values do not have to be communicated in writing.

Whichever approach is taken in building an organizational culture that supports high levels of employee satisfaction, several key elements are needed. An employee-centric culture must focus on trust, communication and transparency, empowerment and innovation, and fun.

The Prestwick House Approach

Prestwick House Culture

I HAVE TO START OUT this section by first saying how odd it is to try to discuss a culture you're living in at the moment. Looking for words to express what makes Prestwick House culture unique, I feel a bit like an archeologist might after exploring these offices a thousand years from now with a pick-axe and a flashlight. Trying to explain our culture, the scientist might tell the world, "They ate Lean Cuisine® for lunch!"

or, "They used a trivia game for new-employee orientation!" But those kinds of observations don't really capture what it's like to work here in the present. Because culture is more than just a company's policies, practices, and norms of behavior, it would take a million of those types of details to begin to describe what it's like to work in any given company.

but they are just a few of the many ways
be achieved.

Trust

There is a good business case for building a high level of trust in an organization[2]. As evidenced in a 2002 Watson Wyatt study, trust can translate into greater profit, having an impact on an organization's bottom-line results. The report by Watson Wyatt suggests that in high-trust organizations, the return to shareholders is three times that of low trust organizations[3]. Retention is also higher in high-trust organizations. And this doesn't just apply to employees; customers are also retained at higher levels.

It is impossible to escape the fact that trust impacts nearly every element in an organization, including, ultimately, the customer. Trust is essential in building relationships that are necessary for success. In organizations with high-trust cultures, information flows freely, creating a collaborative environment and encouraging employees to openly share with one another. Communication is honest and enables people to address conflict.

Communication and Transparency

Management must consciously choose transparency. That is, they must choose to be open and honest—at all times, and they must be open to both positive and negative information. There are no degrees of transparency; either the company is transparent or it isn't. Holding anything back, misleading, keeping secrets, or even omitting information are not the actions of a transparent organization. There is a ripple effect that carries the attitudes of managers down to employees and, from there, to the customer. If communication is open and candid, it will ultimately shape the customer experience.

In the twenty-first century, the need for honesty and candor has become even more important. Organizations must be ever mindful, as information becomes increasingly accessible to all through the expansion of the Internet, that their actions may be leaving an eternal and wide-reaching footprint—perhaps forever highlighting incidents of dishonesty.

Open, honest communication begins with consistency. Sharing what you know, when you know it, is greatly appreciated by employees—even if it's bad news. Withholding bad news destroys trust. Of course, it's okay to say that you don't know—if you really don't know—but you must agree to share when you do know.

Communication must be continuous, and formal interactions must be supplemented with informal exchanges. Constant feedback to employees is critical. Frequent one-on-one sessions with employees and team or departmental meetings will help keep channels of communication open, while also providing an opportunity for employees to clarify expectations and objectives.

Management must, however, engage in two-way communication, encouraging feedback and even constructive dissent. This requires that management truly be ready to listen, and, when appropriate, take action in response to feedback, acknowledging that employees have been heard.

The Prestwick House Approach
to Trust, Communications, and Transparency

OUR FINANCIALS ARE AN OPEN BOOK, at Prestwick House. We talk about our P&L and where we stand from a sales and expense perspective on a monthly basis, and all general ledger accounts other than payroll are open to everyone in the company on an ongoing basis. Everyone has a clear picture of what things cost and what our sales figures are on an ongoing basis. People know how much money is flowing into the employee bonus account at any given time, as well as how much we are being charged for rent.

But that's simple, entry-level transparency. On a deeper level, at Prestwick House, trust and transparency has to do with limiting and, where possible, eliminating sub-text. We are constantly working to build a system in which employees trust management to make good, informed decisions, and management trusts employees to bring a high level of energy and creativity to their jobs. Having that level of trust between employees and the company means we don't have to burden the operation with perfunctory corporate policies geared to managing the underperformers.

But that level of trust also means that I get questioned on expenses and

the environment.

However, many employees have expressed concerns about the idea of making this purchase in 2009—a year in which we have seen major cuts to basic hygiene factors like compensation, benefits, and job security, including:

- 0% pay increases and talk of possible reductions
- elimination of major benefits like tuition reimbursement and talk of further benefit reductions
- elimination of the part-time customer service position and discussions of possible layoffs for other staff members

With this in mind, we think it would be detrimental to employee morale to make this purchase at such a critical time in the lives of the company and its employees. Therefore, the suggestion has been made that we delay the purchase of the solar panels until the company is back on track to provide pay increases and full benefits to all employees.

* I.D.E.A. is an acronym for Inter-Departmental Employee Advisory Committee. It is a group that was put together to meet once a month to develop some practical and achievable goals for Prestwick House to work towards over the next 52 weeks that will increase employee satisfaction and advance us toward our goal of being the best place to work in Delaware. In practice, it has become a way for employees to communicate concerns to upper management; the committee acts a sort of suggestion box or advocacy group for employees.

This email was sent to me by members of the current year's I.D.E.A. Committee. The I.D.E.A. (Inter-Departmental Employee Advisory) Committee is part of an array of communications and transparency tools we devised to make sure we were constantly in touch with any simmering staff concerns.

I have to admit that I was taken aback by this email from the committee. But, as I searched my memory for what I might have said that could have caused concern among the staff, I realized that I probably could have been clearer in my explanation of the solar-panel purchase. With that in mind, I sent out the following email in response:

Subject: Solar Project Clarification

I want to thank the I.D.E.A. committee for bringing the fact that my remarks at some of the strategic planning meetings about the solar energy project were unclear.

Here is where the project stands:

The project has been scaled down to $20,000. That is pretty cheap for a $59,000 system, once tax rebates and subsidies are factored in. However, in view of the budget constraints that we are operating under this year, even $20,000 is not an amount we would spend lightly. Nevertheless, it makes sense to think about making the purchase this year, since subsidies and tax rebates for this type of project will be reduced over the next few years, as demand for these systems increases.

One possible way to finance the project this year would be to have Jim (the owner of this building) purchase the system by taking out an ordinary bank loan. We are currently looking into that option. I hope that it will work because that option would provide long-term economic benefits to the company without diminishing our budget. If that option does not work, for whatever reason, we will not be going forward with the solar project this year, since we have not budgeted for loan payments, and we are committed to restricting our operating expenses this year.

For another example of transparency at Prestwick House, we can look at the way we handled a difficult situation in the past. In 2005, we had

hired additional staff and ramped up a project that, for a number of reasons, did not work out. We were able to let go of employees that were
working on the failed project and make the case for this move in a very
direct way that would make sense to everyone involved. In this situation,
we found that, because we were open from the beginning of the ven-

believe that we will uphold the

established. By declaring our intention of being a great place to work,
we've put our management decisions under intense scrutiny. Everyone in
the company is aware of management's commitment to that goal, so we
run the risk of losing credibility if our actions fall short of our ideals.

Empowerment and Innovation

It is management's responsibility to create a culture that allows employees
to be self-motivated. According to Lior Arussy in *Excellence Every Day: Make
the Daily Choice—Inspire Your Employees and Amaze Your Customers*, management must create an "excellence-enabling environment."[4] Management,
then, must provide employees with the tools, resources, and freedom that will
empower them to perform. This means using a minimum of restrictive rules
and procedures. Otherwise, you are likely to have a herd of sheep, blindly
following and passively obeying rules, rather than having employees who
take initiative and think creatively. Employees must be empowered to take
charge and perform at superior levels. The leadership of the organization cannot mandate commitment. Managers have to let go of control and decrease
their focus on the rules.

In a culture of excellence, "good" work is simply not good enough. The
key is to inspire employees to go beyond "good" and beyond their comfort
zones. Employees must take personal responsibility and assume a sense of
ownership for their work. They must ultimately understand their impact on

customers and others in the organization. This empowerment requires that employees are knowledgeable about the business and the customers. The foundation for this is a clear statement of the company's mission, objectives, and expectations.

Management, then, must focus on the people, not the process. The old, traditional style of management focused on processes and procedures—controlling employees. Yet today, "process cannot be the ultimate goal" as Arussy puts it[5]. Managers must empower employees by letting them customize processes, so as to deliver superior customer service.

In the old management approach, a paycheck bought the company a mechanical level of performance from employees. But we now recognize that financial rewards do not capture the hearts and minds of workers, and that by failing to inspire, we leave incredible untapped potential on the table. Employees will only be comfortable with innovation in a culture that allows them to trust and be trusted by management. With a relationship built on trust, employees are comfortable taking risks. This means that management does not punish failures when employees take calculated risks for the good of the organization. In fact, an innovative environment *encourages* risk taking.

The Prestwick House Approach
to Empowerment and Innovation

AN EMPLOYEE-SATISFACTION CULTURE BEGINS with people being satisfied with their actual jobs. In our experience, money can compensate for having a terrible job, but only for a short time. After that, the most lavish company benefits and perks shrink into invisibility if you don't enjoy the work. So, in addition to making sure that the right person is hired and in place, it's important to make sure that each job we offer is rewarding and satisfying.

How do we make packing boxes or taking customer calls rewarding, nourishing, enriching?

At Prestwick House we start with making sure everyone has a clear picture of the company's goals and a clear sense that each individual has a responsibility to help us meet those goals. The upshot is that each employee understands that his or her job is not simply to put books in boxes, but to help the company meet its goals.

For example, during the summer, which is when we receive most of our orders, I sometimes help out in the warehouse, packing boxes. Just before I left for lunch one day this summer, I picked up a carton of books that had a damaged corner. I assumed that one or two of the books inside the box might have been damaged—and we try to never send out damaged products.

On this specific occasion, right before lunch, I placed the box on the

Fun

Taking the advice of Stephen C. Lundin, John Christensen, and Harry Paul in the Fish! Philosophy, we can be serious about business, without abandoning the idea of having fun and creating an environment that people will enjoy[6]. Energy and enthusiasm abound in such an environment, as we can see in the example of Zappos.com. Zappos has taken Lundin, Christensen, and Paul's advice to heart—and in so doing has earned a place on *Fortune's* list of "Best Companies to Work For". Coming in at number 23 in 2009, the online retailer has created a culture that nurtures the creative, childlike side of its employees, while absolutely delighting its customers. Zappos's CEO, Tony Hsieh, wanted to ensure that he created a culture where people would not dread going to work, and he has succeeded. To maintain such a culture while experiencing incredible growth, however, has required particular attention to recruitment. According to Hsieh, it's a mistake and a kind of compromise to simply "fill seats with warm bodies."[7]

The policies that maintain Zappos's unique culture may seem somewhat unusual to more traditional firms. The company encourages their managers to spend time getting to know employees—beyond just time shared in the office. Employees are also empowered to give each other $50 bonuses. Even the company's interview and application process reflect their somewhat quirky culture. Zappos has hit upon a system that works for them and their unique strategy, and they provide a perfect illustration of the need to customize processes to fit each specific organization and its culture[8].

Libby Sartain was clear in articulating this need when she rolled out the values statement for Yahoo! entitled "What Sucks!" She felt that this cynical approach to communicating what Yahoo! stood for would work for their employees. It would not, however, work for the majority of organizations. Sartain took the time to learn the culture and identify the approach that would be best received by Yahoo!'s staff[9]. There is no "one size fits all" approach; it is critical to customize.

The Prestwick House Approach
to Fun

AS A MANAGER, I CAME OF AGE in the middle of the dot-com bubble, when workers were forced by their employers to attend mandatory "company fun" weekend events. Imagine ocean kayaking at 8:30 am, followed by beach volley ball at 11:00, followed by brainstorming over lunch. I'm not exaggerating. If getting up early on Saturday and spending the day with your boss in a sand-filled bathing suit playing volley ball and pretending to have fun does not sound pleasant to you, congratulations—you are a normal human being.

We avoid forced fun, at Prestwick House**. I've always preferred the kind of organic fun I found working in the National Endowment for the Arts, where sitting around and talking to interesting, active people who watched interesting movies and read interesting books took up much of the office's downtime.

That's why at Prestwick House, we don't have lifeless, routine birthday parties or paintball outings. Instead, there's a general atmosphere that encourages "easy-goingness" and camaraderie every day. Rather than trying to graft fun events onto an otherwise boring workweek, we try to have fun along the way as we work. Every Tuesday and Thursday at lunchtime, many of us can be found playing poker in the café. On any hour of the workday Prestwick House staff can be seen enjoying each other's company, demonstrating that it is fun to work when you're with people you like and respect.

** Most corporate "team building" and forced fun events I've heard of appeal to a specific type of outgoing, gregarious type of employee. That might be because they are developed by outgoing and gregarious HR professionals & CEOs who think that their idea of "fun" is shared by all. At Prestwick House, we try not to make that assumption.

Being an educational publisher, we also have the opportunity to have a little fun by using our staff members as models for our book covers. The photos below show a few of our employees posing for a cover.

At Prestwick House, we like to keep the focus on having this kind of spontaneous fun along the way, rather than kind of contrived, corporate-sanctioned fun one often sees in the business world.

Exceptions to the Rule

Having said that, I should also mention that there are two "forced fun" events of the year: Prestwick House Jeopardy and the annual Christmas Party.

The Christmas party allows us the opportunity to have fun, while also creating a sense of tradition, which helps reinforce some aspects of the company's unique culture. One rite of passage that everyone looks forward is an annual song or skit performed by the "Song Committee," comprised of all the new employees hired that year. This tradition was borrowed from the public relations firm of Porter Novelli, where my wife worked years ago. Each year, new staff members are informed when they are hired that they are now a member of the current year's Song Committee, and that they will have to work with the other new people hired that year, from all levels of the company, to come up with some form of entertainment for the Christmas party.

Traditionally, this group begins to fret in October and gets very nervous in November, but by Christmas, they've always come through with a song or a sketch that is full of inside jokes and leaves all the spouses and significant others in attendance scratching their heads, while we all laugh.

The other regular tradition is the annual awards presentation. This is an opportunity to humorously (one hopes) thank each employee for the behind-the-scenes role that he or she fills. There are a million little factors within each job that help make the company work, and I try to bring attention to those items and thank each individual.

The party is a fun and mostly painless team-building activity, and to date, it has always been a huge success. And it isn't only me saying that—caterers who have helped with the Christmas party have commented that they have never seen a group have as much fun as we do.

Another new-hire orientation activity is "Prestwick House Jeopardy," a game that tests rookies and veterans alike on trivia related to Prestwick House. When a new hire comes on, I try to find something interesting about him or her that might not come up in the course of an ordinary conversation. For example, "Have you ever been bitten by a poisonous snake?" or, "Did you play an instrument in high school?"

In addition to the "Prestwick House Peeps" category, we ask questions that reinforce points of policy, procedure and company lore. ✿

The Employee Satisfaction
REVOLUTION

Organizational Culture

• Satisfied Customers
• Low Turnover
• High Productivity
• Recruitment Advantage
• Financial Success

Bottom Line

Employee Statisfaction

Organizational Culture
• Trust
• Communication
• Empowerment
• Fun

Leadership
• Strategic Planning
• Ethics
• Authentic Leadership
• Transparency

HR Strategies
• Work/Life Balance
• Recruitment
• Employee Motivation
• Training & Development
• Performance Appraisals

"Employee satisfaction impacts the bottom line and is largely determined by employee day-to-day interactions with managers. Of all the factors an organization can improve to impact employee satisfaction, improving individual leadership is the most effective."

MICHAEL LEIMBACH[1]

TOO MUCH EMPHASIS HAS BEEN PLACED on temporary sources by which companies gain a short-lived advantage over the competition. Today, we must consider sources that can provide a more sustainable competitive advantage. Value is added to the organization largely through and by its employees.

Research by Wilson Learning Worldwide has suggested that nearly 40% of a company's bottom-line performance can be attributed to the job satisfaction of employees—and this is directly related to the leadership skills of the managers[2]. Managing a company involves very specifically identifying how they lead their people. The importance of leaders and the role they play in promoting job satisfaction cannot be underestimated.

Authentic Leadership

Organizational leadership plays a crucial role in employee satisfaction. A study by Susan M. Jensen and Fred Luthans found that employees' perceptions of their organization's management as authentic leaders was one of the best predictors of an employee's level of both commitment and satisfaction[3]. This is particularly important for smaller organizations, where the founder of a relatively new business is actively involved in the operations of the firm. The perception that he or she is an authentic leader can have a profound impact on employee attitudes. Furthermore, when employees' attitudes are positive, there is likely to be a similar positive impact on customer satisfaction and the overall growth of the company. The impact of an authentic leader can be leveraged to great advantage in a firm.

It is often said that attitudes are contagious, and it makes sense that leaders who have high levels of job satisfaction will work to ensure that their employees are also satisfied. And the end result will likely be a more satisfied customer.

Old School versus New School

The traditional view of leadership suggests that a subordinate's role is to serve his or her leaders. This view is certainly outdated and ineffective in today's business environment. The current view of leadership—one that is quite effective—suggests a role reversal; today's leaders must serve their employees. As Arussy reminds us in *Excellence Every Day*, leaders "are at the service of [their] employees."[4] As many have discovered, there is true power in learning how to serve others. When employees work in an encouraging environment, the affirmation they receive is then reflected in their customer interactions. The customer experiences that positivity and ultimately reaps its benefits. Positive employees *want* to meet their customers' needs.

However, this kind of environment does not happen by accident. Leadership practices that increase employee satisfaction include aligning individual employee performance with the organization's mission and objectives; delivering feedback to employees on how they are progressing towards their goals; supplying the tools necessary for employees to perform well and succeed; and offering development opportunities for employees. (Note: More details on these HR strategies will be presented in Chapter 7.)

The traditional management approach was about managing through control. New-school management, by contrast, is about nurturing. Managers must continually ask "Why should they trust me?" The old-school manager thinks that trust is due simply to his or her position in the organization. But the modern manager knows that it is his or her responsibility to earn trust. The conventional management approach uses fear, while the new uses respect. Inspiration has replaced control as a preferred tool of the new breed of managers. It naturally follows that effective leadership today requires a unique set of competencies.

While there is certainly no definite "one size fits all" approach to organi-

and, since a business requires a broad skill set to be successful, leaders must be astute enough to surround themselves with those who possess complementary skill sets. The author of *The Contrarian's Guide to Leadership*, Steven Sample, advises leaders to compensate for their own weaknesses by hiring others who are indeed stronger[5].

Being self-aware has additional benefits for leaders today. When we are more self-aware, we are better able to understand others—and their responses to us as leaders. Learning about others begins with learning about oneself.

A great deal of emphasis has been placed on emotional intelligence in today's workforce. The increasingly popular view is that emotional intelligence is more important than general IQ as a key competency[6]. Daniel Goleman's has been a strong proponent of this idea; in a book that he co-authored, called *Primal Leadership*, he stressed the crucial role emotional intelligence plays in making a good leader. According to Goleman, when leaders possess self-control and are able to manage their emotions, they are better able to understand the emotions of others[7].

Being a Role Model
Leaders must model the kinds of behaviors they expect of others throughout the organization. The days of, "Do as I say, not as I do" in the business world are over. Employees carefully observe a leader for clues about how they should act. Modeling behaviors, then, becomes essential as leaders lead nonverbally. Behaviors communicate volumes as others watch—and decide whether or not to follow.

John Maxwell takes a clear stance on this issue in his book *The 360 Degree Leader*, which emphasizes the importance of leading by example. According to Maxwell, those who quietly lead by example are respected by others[8].

The Role of Curiosity in Leadership

Adaptability is another key competency for effective modern leaders. Leaders cannot drive the change process so critical to business today without a natural curiosity and willingness to improvise. Those who are wedded to the past are doomed to failure, but naturally curious leaders are life-long learners who encourage their employees to develop and grow as well. With a commitment to learning, leaders are able to improve both themselves and their organizations.

The development of an organization's vision hinges, to a large extent, on the leadership's natural curiosity. When leaders are too grounded in the past, they often find it difficult to provide a clear sense of direction. And it is only with a clear understanding of the direction of the firm that employees can become deeply involved. If employees do not understand their company's objectives and goals, it is virtually impossible for them to participate fully. Furthermore, it is critical that each individual understands how his or her own goals and responsibilities are related to the overall strategic objectives of the firm. This knowledge provides the foundation for each employee's commitment to the organization.

Leaders who are curious are able to encourage others to be similarly curious, to take risks, and to challenge the status quo. Empowering others enables leaders to create a fulfilling environment.

The Courage to Let Go

Empowering others requires courage. It is often difficult, and sometimes even painful, to nurture others, only to watch as they challenge what we have built. And yet, this is exactly how organizations are transformed. Courageous leaders should, therefore, encourage others to take risks. This requires, though, that the leadership be able to embrace both the successes and the failures that result. Since not every experiment or new idea will work, mistakes must not be punished. While not all managers may be comfortable with a "mistake of the month" program as Arussy describes[9], it is important to carefully acknowledge mistakes.

Leaders today must pay particular attention to how they empower their employees. One astute manager I know has very bravely stated that his responsibility was simply to hire good people and then "get out of their way" and let them do what they were hired to do. Part of this responsibility also involves getting rid of any barriers to their performance. Leaders might be seen as having the additional role of clearing any roadblocks for their employees if organizational processes and procedures are creating unnecessary obstacles to performance.

Open-Book Leadership

the books is, however, just one step towards building an ownership culture.

Open-book management was popularized when Jack Stack engineered the turn-around of Springfield Manufacturing Corporation using this approach. His decision to open up the books to employees in the early 1980s was the beginning of one of the best recovery stories in business history. Before long, large companies were inspired to take the open-book approach that had long been practiced by smaller organizations. This technique enables employees and managers to view themselves as being on the same team—in order to score a "win" for the organization, both must work together.

Empowerment of employees means little if they don't have access to the same information that management has. It's hard to imagine employees making the "best" business decisions if they don't have all the information. Yet simply providing the financial information is not sufficient; employees must also be trained in reading the financials and using this information effectively. This education should include an overview of the industry, including the general external environment within which the company operates, and the company's strategy. This, then, provides a framework for understanding company-specific information.

Open communication means having an ongoing discussion of the mission and vision of the organization. A clear understanding of the company's purpose and direction is required if employees are to contribute their talents to the achievement of organizational objectives.

The Prestwick House Approach

to Leadership

PRESTWICK HOUSE IS CONSTANTLY WORKING to foster a "self-managed" approach to every job, and we avoid creating management processes that require us to be constantly looking over people's shoulders. It should, therefore, come as no surprise that we don't emphasize the traditional, capital 'L' style of leadership.

As a company, we reject the typical business-school vision of leadership that depicts leaders with square jaws, standing heroically on an outcropping of rocks, peering off into the horizon. In fact, over the years, I have come to the conclusion that it is a terrible shame that engineers like Henry Ford and Frederick Taylor invented the field of modern human resources. They set the bar awfully low by treating labor as just another interchangeable input.

Our cultural view of leadership has, to a large degree, been poisoned by the early industrialists, who built a system in which all decisios were pushed up the chain of command to an elite, decision-making class. It was they—not the workers—who did all the thinking about how each job should be done. In fact, Taylor famously said that anybody who had the physically ability to handle pig iron could not also have the mental capacity to think about how to handle pig iron. Indeed, we in the "post-smokestack" era of industry have quite a challenge to contend with in undoing the damage that the early industrialists' thinking has done to labor-management relations.

At Prestwick House, we look to the example of more modern leaders, like Nvidia's Jen-Hsun Huang. In a Stanford University Podcast on entrepreneurship*, Huang commented that he doesn't even like the term "leadership" because it sounds like a quality that only certain people are blessed with. Huang said that he thinks more in terms of "perspective" than leadership. Everyone has a perspective, and anyone who trusts his or her perspective can be a leader.

A surprising case study that illustrates the kind of leadership Huang describes can be found in Carol Burnett.

---

* This incredible resource is available at http://ecorner.stanford.edu/authorMaterialInfo.html?mid=2221

I liked the *Carroll Burnett Show* when I was a kid, but I had not paid much attention to her as a person, and I certainly never thought of her as a kind of leadership guru—that is, not until I heard her tell the story of how she got her start in show business. Burnett tells about the time she spent living in New York at "The Rehearsal Club," a boarding house for aspiring actresses. She and many other talented young women from

on a show that was wildly successful. From there, Burnett signed with the William Morris Agency, and her career was off to a promising start.

I love that story, and Carroll Burnett's telling of it made me love her as a leader. We see in this story that you don't have to bully anyone into cooperating with you, if the clarity and simplicity of your vision speaks for itself. It's a story about trusting one's own insight and perspective.

Executives Executing

Having spoken negatively about "old school" leadership, we should also acknowledge that part of building transparency and trust in an organization is being visible in the role of the executive. All companies need a final arbiter who can make difficult decisions when necessary. That is an important part of the executive's job.

At Prestwick House, there have been quite a few situations that have called for strong executive leadership. For example, in 2005, we had to shut down a failing division. We knew that livelihoods were at stake, but we acted directly and didn't hesitate to make the best decision for the company. So, while we try to be inclusive, there are clearly some situations that don't lend themselves to a democratic decision-making process—and people understand and accept that.

Here, we can draw an analogy to the way pirate ships worked, as Peter T. Leeson does in *The Invisible Hook: The Hidden Economics of Pirates*. Leeson notes that on a pirate ship, the captain was, for the most part, equal in status to the other men on the ship, and that it was only during times of crisis that he took on a true executive role. Leeson writes of the pirate captain,

"his one unique power was absolute command during battle; in this way, pirates got the advantage of quick decisions from a powerful commander and total obedience from his fighters when the heat of battle was upon them, while enjoying the leisurely indulgence of deliberation and voting when things were calmer."[10]

That is what we try to do, and that perspective has helped us increase employee satisfaction because, while we are an organization that is progressive in a lot of ways, people in all organizations want clarity and decisiveness during difficult situations.

But those moments of "battle" are few and far between. Prestwick House encourages predicable, daily service in its leaders, and not the swashbuckling, "courageous" style of leadership that everyone hears so much about, which is less than useless to an organization 95% of the time.

The Ironic Downside of this Kind of Leadership

Unfortunately, all of this trust and transparency has its drawbacks—if you are the kind of person who needs to be constantly congratulated for being a great leader, you might want to stick to the old scientific-management practices.

If a company lacks the classical, highly visible executive, and employees can be found making a lot of decisions on their own, people natural devalue the leader's impact on the organization.

When viewed through the classical leadership paradigms, letting people figure out how to solve problems and setting them loose to pursue goals that they have themselves established doesn't seem like leadership at all. This was a revelation that hit me in the gut when we first started taking part in local and national "best place to work" surveys. Our lowest scores were, and continue to be, in the leadership category.

I have struggled with that a bit. After all, I worked for years to put a system in place that people seemed to love. We scored high on quality of work life, on benefits, and on mission, but we fared poorly in the "quality of leadership" category. I couldn't figure it out.

Being human, my first reaction to reading the survey abstracts (you don't get individual surveys to protect employees' confidentiality) was angry disappointment. However, after giving myself a few minutes to cool down, I realized that the responses made sense in the context of the culture we were trying to establish. I was also inspired to make some changes that would improve the company, like the formation of the I.D.E.A. Committee, which I've mentioned previously.

Department-Level Leadership
The bottom line is that Prestwick House-style leadership is not glamor-

_____

_____
_____
_____
_____
_____

Addendum for Managers Self-Evaluations   Name: _____

I provide my staff with meaningful feedback throughout the year.

Disagree Strongly	Disagree	Agree	Agree Strongly
0	0	0	0

In the past six months I have provided the following staff members meaningful feedback:

_____
_____
_____

(Attach up to 1 additional sheet if necessary)

I praise the work of my staff in front of other managers, other staff members, or the rest of the company.

Disagree Strongly	Disagree	Agree	Agree Strongly
0	0	0	0

I have praised the following staff members:

_____
_____
_____

(Attach up to 1 additional sheet if necessary)

I have modeled honesty and integrity to my staff.

Disagree Strongly	Disagree	Agree	Agree Strongly
0	0	0	0

The following is an instance where I have modeled honesty and integrity:

_____

_____

_____

(Attach up to 1 additional sheet if necessary)

I have provided my staff with clear career paths that includes milestones and requirements for advancement.

Disagree Strongly	Disagree	Agree	Agree Strongly
0	0	0	0

I have had the career path conversation with the following staff members:

_____

_____

_____

(Attach up to 1 additional sheet if necessary)

I have demonstrated to my staff that I trust them to take independent action.

Disagree Strongly	Disagree	Agree	Agree Strongly
0	0	0	0

The following independent actions have been taken by staff members:

_____

_____

_____

(Attach up to 1 additional sheet if necessary)

I have managed my department with fairness and without favoritism.

Disagree Strongly	Disagree	Agree	Agree Strongly
0	0	0	0

My staff would say that there is a high degree of procedural justice in the department.

Disagree Strongly	Disagree	Agree	Agree Strongly
0	0	0	0

This self-evaluation is based specifically on promoting employee satisfaction. Managers are encouraged to view their staff members as their customers, so the manager's evaluation basically asks, "Are you providing your customers with great service?"

Parting Thoughts on Leadership

LIFE BALANCE, AND RECRUITING

The Employee Satisfaction
REVOLUTION

- Satisfied Customers
- Low Turnover
- High Productivity
- Recruitment Advantage
- Financial Success

Organizational Culture

Bottom Line

Employee Statisfaction

Leadership
- Strategic Planning
- Ethics
- Authentic Leadership
- Transparency

Organizational Culture
- Trust
- Communication
- Empowerment
- Fun

HR Strategies
- Work/Life Balance
- Recruitment
- Employee Motivation
- Training & Development
- Performance Appraisals

*"No matter the industry, HR strategies can
and do affect company financial performance
and employee satisfaction."*

GEVITY-CORNELL UNIVERSITY STUDY[1]

E VEN WITH AN IDEAL ORGANIZATIONAL CULTURE and leaders who say all the right
things, a company must take care to employ the proper human resource
strategies. While we will discuss each of these HR strategies individually in
this chapter, it is critical to recognize that even greater results can be achieved
by using all of them together.

The Importance of Intangible Benefits

Alex Edmans's research has highlighted the importance of intangibles in our
organizations and the ironic failure of the stock market to fully value them.
In examining Fortune's "100 Best Companies to Work for in America" from
1998 to 2005, Edmans found above-average returns for these "best" companies. These "100 best" companies were performing at an average of 14%, as
compared to the overall market performance of 6%. As a result, Edmans has

challenged the traditional management approach of "treating workers like any other input."[2] The traditional approach he describes involves using money as the primary motivator for employees. But, simply put, that doesn't work today. Money can be a short-term motivator, but job satisfaction has been more and more widely recognized as a key to motivating employees in the modern workforce.

Furthermore, Edmans's research highlights the problem of short-term thinking demonstrated by managers throughout Corporate America. Even those managers who have accepted the theory that employee satisfaction will positively impact the organization's long-term performance don't necessarily follow through with the appropriate actions, partly because the financial investments in our employees' satisfaction can have a negative impact on a company's financial records in the short-term. This, in turn, may negatively impact the manager's compensation and opportunities for advancement.

Managers have repeatedly voiced concerns that investors would not accept lower profits in a given financial period in exchange for an investment in employee satisfaction that may reap benefits in the future. Investing in our employees, however, does pay off in a variety of critical arenas, some of which may not show up in economic results right away. As Edmans suggests, "...significant components of a firm's value cannot be captured by accounting numbers."[3] With this in mind, forward-thinking managers should recognize the intangible value of a satisfied workforce.

Employee Motivation: Creating Positive Feedback Loops and Eliminating Morale Killers

While both tangible and intangible benefits can result from effectively motivating the workforce, we should also keep in mind that there are costs associated with a de-motivated and disengaged workforce. Disgruntled employees are more likely to be guilty of theft, sabotage, lost productivity, or poor customer service.

Those managers who find themselves unable to motivate others may find themselves unable to manage effectively. The way people are managed will impact their commitment to an organization and its objectives. Most workers usually don't exert the greatest possible effort—and some have estimated that employees generally work at little more than half of their potential. The million dollar question is how to get employees to expend that last 40%.

Scientific management was the early approach to the motivation of employees. Frederick Taylor, the "father" of this method, presented workers as simply extensions of the machines they operated, and thought that their motivations were primarily economic. Management theory has evolved significantly since then, but companies have not necessarily kept pace. Although it's been nearly a century since Elton Mayo ushered in the human relations movement at the Hawthorne Western Electric plant, some organizations still have not recognized the importance of non-economic motivators.

The reinforcement literature is clear in suggesting that positive reinforce-

Managers, then, must be trained in how to administer punishments, when appropriate, that include a specific discussion on how an employee can improve.

Each individual is driven by a different set of needs, and there is no universal approach that works in motivating employees. The key is flexibility. Effective managers will possess a mixed bag of motivational tools and know how to align each with the needs of individual employees.

Companies invest heavily in their IT and equipment. But what about the tools to motivate employees? As the workforce changes, the motivational techniques we use must also change to keep pace. Unfortunately, organizations more often take the easy way out. Instead of being creative and identifying new approaches to motivating today's employees, they use old, time-worn techniques—and then wonder why their approach doesn't work. Or they simply say that they don't have an adequate budget.

Successful motivation requires active participation by managers; they must get to know their employees so they can design motivational incentives appropriate to each. Inspiring a workforce is not always a function of budget. A simple "thank you" or an encouraging word costs nothing, but can be a great motivator.

---

[*] This propensity to use punishment has created a need for books like *The Carrot Principle* and *A Carrot a Day*, which remind business people to use positive reinforcement.

Lateral moves have replaced "the fast track" in organizations today. High-performing employees today are more likely to be rewarded with a zigzag pattern of movement throughout the organization rather than with an upward promotion. These lateral moves reward employees with new challenges and communicate to employees that they are valued. Lateral movement can reinforce the willingness of the company to continue their investment in employees.

Creating an environment in which employees can be self-motivated and self-managed is critical. HR strategies that allow employees to manage themselves are critical. In the information age, much of the workforce is made up of knowledge workers"—experts who want to be empowered to decide how their jobs can best be performed. Such employees usually do not need, or want, close supervision. Micro-management wastes valuable resources, not the least of which are the time and talent of managers and the opportunity for employee growth and creativity. The ultimate loser in this game is the organization.

Recognition is a critical factor in motivating employees, and some studies have even identified it as the number one motivator"". Even so, most companies do not even have a systematic process for thanking employees. This is becoming even more critical as a new Generation Y is entering the workforce. These younger workers are escaping the fear tactics and threats that were routine for the Baby Boomers—the traditional approach to management. The newest entrants to the workforce seem to be looking for a likeable boss and a positive work climate[4]. The rewards system is a critical part of building such an environment.

Most individuals enjoy being part of a winning team. If they know they have made contributions to a group's success, it's even better. Providing feedback to employees can be an effective way to make them feel that they are part of an organization's successes.

It would seem that the various ways in which companies approach motivation can provide great insight into what they really value. Those companies that believe that employees can be easily replaced don't place much emphasis on motivation. When their employees are burned out, they simply hire new ones. This practice not only sends a dangerous message to the workforce,

[**] Popularized by Peter Drucker, this term underscores the importance of knowledge and expertise in the modern business world.

[***] Just one of the many early reports that reinforce this point is Shari Cauldron's "The Top 20 Ways to Motivate Employees" (*Industry Week*, April 3, 1995, pp. 15-16).

but it also incurs a high cost for the organization, through the additional training and hiring costs caused by a high turnover rate. Wise leaders, however, realize that employees can take the same approach—those who do not feel valued can just as easily replace their employers.

Recruitment: Getting the Right People on the Bus

Employee selection is critical in any organization, and with talent management topping the list of most organizations' strategic challenges, companies must begin by addressing recruitment and selection. It's all about getting the right people on the bus and in the right seat, and letting those who are no longer needed get off at the next stop.

Retail organizations participating in a survey have reported an amazing 75% reduction in turnover when they have considered person-organization alignment in the selection process, emphasized self-management approaches, and built a more family-oriented work environment[5]. Employee-selection practices must involve hiring the right person the first time, and the best managers would rather leave a position unfilled if the proper candidate cannot be found. Rushing to fill the position just doesn't work. Identifying the best candidate for a position requires much more today than simply finding someone who's willing to give it a try.

The most progressive organizations go beyond person-job fit; that is, they do more than just match the skill sets of job applicants with the requirements of a job description. One of the most important items to consider, beyond person-job fit, is person-organization fit—the alignment of the individual with the organization's culture and values and with the rest of the company's employees. Companies have achieved greater financial growth and significantly lower employee turnover when they have considered person-organization fit in the selection process. In addition, managers must take a future-oriented view when hiring, considering not just whether the candidate can perform the job today, but also whether he or she fits well with the culture of the firm and is likely to make contributions to the organization well into the future.

When hiring, managers should pay particular attention to ensure that candidates are self-motivated and possess values that are closely aligned with those of the organization. For example, a customer-service oriented culture should seek out individuals who care about customer service and possess the internal motivation to deliver superior performance. Managers must fight the temptation to select the candidates who are most like them, instead hiring applicants with complementary skill sets.

Realistic job previews ("RJPs") are another important part of making better hiring decisions. The company's credibility is at stake if managers present unrealistic expectations of a job, only to reveal the truth after a candidate has accepted their offer. Meanwhile, the company may have missed out on a candidate who would have been a good fit for the job, as it actually is.

Once a candidate is selected, it is important that he or she be effectively oriented to the organization—especially its culture and values. Those high-performing organizations that emphasize customer service must begin the acculturation process from day one, with a formal orientation or on-boarding process that communicates what the company expects.

Work/Life Balance: Exploring the Intangible Benefits Package

Above all else, companies today must remember that flexibility is essential. With increasing diversity in the workplace, it will be increasingly important to accommodate a wide range of needs and values.

Work/life programs are one way of accommodating different types of employees, and, while the actual financial cost of work/life programs is relatively low, the benefits can be substantial. These benefits may be both tangible and intangible.

The need for work/life balance has never been greater in American businesses than it is now, as the workforce seeks out and demands more flexibility. A workplace with a good work/life balance is better able to attract and retain talent. A survey conducted by Workplace Options reveals that over 40% of employees are not satisfied with their employer's attention to work/life balance[6]. Companies must be very careful of the blurring of the lines between work and home. Technology has enabled employees to keep in touch with work while vacationing and check company email on weekends. Some employers expect their workers to be available nearly 24/7, simply because the technology exists to allow it.

The younger generations, however, do not value long work hours; neither do they want their work responsibilities to encroach on their personal lives. Younger workers are especially protective of their personal time. Having seen their parents laid off from organizations, they don't feel the same sense of loyalty to their companies as did previous generations. They respond much more favorably to those organizations that give them space and allow them to be themselves in the workplace.

In fact, even workaholic Baby Boomers are now shifting their focus. During their heyday, they felt they were judged on the number of hours worked. Today, this generation is nearing retirement and has a new mindset. Part-time positions that allow them to spend more time with their grandchildren and in leisure activities are important. The opportunity to "try on" retirement is also appealing.

It is the manager's responsibility, with support from the organization, to assist the employee in balancing work and family or personal issues. There is a life outside of the workplace, and it costs nothing for an organization to recognize the existence of an employee's personal life and extend some consideration. Often, the organization will be rewarded with a more loyal and productive employee.

Helping employees achieve a work/life balance doesn't necessarily have to involve grandiose programs and gestures on the organization's part; it can be done through adjusting numerous small details and accommodations. For example, letting employees personalize their workspace with pictures of family or personal knick-knacks allows them to feel more at home.

Work/life programs that can help employees balance their life issues include flexible work arrangements, casual dress, referral services or subsidies for child care and elder care, tuition reimbursement, fitness programs, and sick-child care. Some of the less traditional programs that are growing in popularity include referral services for pet care, legal assistance, financial planning, on-site massage, and convenience services like dry cleaning pick-up.

While the creation of corporate culture was discussed in Chapter 4, a further discussion is warranted here, as it relates to work/life balance. Specifically, creating a family-like environment can be a powerful motivational tool, potentially leading to higher revenue growth and lower employee turnover.

A family-like environment provides an opportunity for employees to get to know one another and to grow comfortable with each other—one of the first steps in generating trust. Those companies that provide social opportunities for employees, openly share information, and hold company-wide meetings achieve great success in this area. Another important component of the family-like environment is a company's profit-sharing plan, and the approach taken in administering it.

The open sharing of information should be two-way; companies foster trust when management openly shares with employees, but equally important is the flow of information from the employees to management. While managers do not have to take specific actions on every recommendation that employees offer, the key is to be sure that management is listening, making reasonable accommodations, and compromising when appropriate.

Today's workforce is concerned with far more than just a paycheck. Those organizations that are proactive in meeting the needs of their workers will address the needs of the whole person, including both work and non-work issues.

Having the right policies is one thing. Ensuring employees don't fear them is quite another. The culture of the organization is important in creating this comfort level.

The Performance Appraisal: How Am I Doing?

The performance appraisal is yet another opportunity for an organization to reinforce to its employees what is important. By rewarding and recognizing those employees who model the appropriate behaviors—those that are reflective of the company's core values—we can also send a message to others in the organization who may not be modeling those behaviors. Therefore, the organization that truly values employee satisfaction and, ultimately, customer satisfaction, must design a performance-appraisal system that clearly reflects this. The entire workforce must be familiar with the evaluation criteria and understand exactly what it means to meet or exceed expectations.

An *Academy of Management Journal* article by David Henderson focuses on the psychological contract between employees and employers, and in particular, on the breaches of these contracts. Henderson's lesson for managers is that they must learn how to manage their own expectations, which is best accomplished by addressing expectations at the outset of the relationship, particularly in the recruitment process. Great care should be taken when making promises to employees. This practice of open communication also extends to the performance appraisal. Employees must know what is expected of them and what the company can expect of them[7].

It is important to create a performance-appraisal system that is supported by management and employees alike, and having an effective system involves providing feedback to employees on their performance. Without an effective evaluation system in place, an organization can experience stagnant employee performance.

Managers must carefully consider what kinds of behaviors and competencies are being evaluated. Performance appraisals should carefully target those aspects of an individual's performance critical to the organization's goals, and, from a legal perspective, only those behaviors that are directly related to the job should be evaluated.

In the move towards more collaborative performance, self-evaluations have grown in popularity. Since the performance-appraisal system is most effective as a two-way process, the evaluation provides an essential opportunity for employees to present their own perspectives. It also provides an excellent starting point for managers, particularly when performance gaps exist.

Managers must be specific in their feedback, providing insightful details about how a given behavior is helpful or harmful. Simply circling a number on an evaluation form means nothing. To ensure that the appropriate behaviors are repeated and inappropriate behaviors are eliminated, managers must share detailed descriptions. While this explicit feedback is not always easy to deliver, the benefits to both the employee and the organization can be great.

Appraisals should identify areas that can be improved through some form of coaching, training, or mentoring. Identifying strengths is also important, as doing so will help the organization build a skills inventory for administrative purposes. Having such records enables a company to identify in-house candidates when new positions open, matching the skill sets required in the available position with the skill set of employees in the skills bank.

Training and Development

Employees can meet performance expectations only if they are provided the necessary tools to be successful. Investing in an organization's workforce is a critical part of improving the overall performance of the firm. An investment in the company's people is an investment in the company's performance.

Assurance Agency is a perfect example of a firm that has used this principle to its advantage. The company keeps employee development and the creation of a fun environment at the top of its list of priorities, with a particular focus on professional development. As Steven Handmaker, VP of Marketing and Communications, says, "We understand that happy and educated employees mean happy clients."[8] At Assurance Agency, education is seen as an important foundation for providing high-quality customer service, as it allows employees to stay informed about their industry and their field. Assurance Agency is clear in communicating that their top goal is to create happy employees. It is those happy employees who drive their customer service success. But employees can achieve this goal only if they are provided with development opportunities and the tools to succeed.

One of the key responsibilities of any company today is to create an environment that encourages employees to continually learn new skills. Organizations should encourage employees to attend conferences, workshops, or even in-house programs. Refreshing established skills and acquiring new ones motivates employees and shows them how much they are valued.

PRESTWICK HOUSE'S
HR STRATEGIES:
COMMUNICATION AND MOTIVATION

The Employee Satisfaction
REVOLUTION

Organizational Culture

- Satisfied Customers
- Low Turnover
- High Productivity
- Recruitment Advantage
- Financial Success

Bottom Line

Employee Statisfaction

Leadership
- Strategic Planning
- Ethics
- Authentic Leadership
- Transparency

Organizational Culture
- Trust
- Communication
- Empowerment
- Fun

HR Strategies
- Work/Life Balance
- Recruitment
- Employee Motivation
- Training & Development
- Performance Appraisals

PRESTWICK HOUSE'S HR STRATEGIES: COMMUNICATION AND MOTIVATION

"I feel like a real part of Prestwick House.
I don't feel that any one person or any department is
seen as less important. We are all an equal factor in
contributing to the company's success."

PRESTWICK HOUSE EMPLOYEE

In the early days, Prestwick House started out with basic, "off the shelf" strategic planning. That is to say, we figured out what the company's core mission was, and then we built a five-year plan that included some stretch goals (for example, becoming the "best place to work in Delaware") based on what we perceived as the company's greatest strengths, weaknesses, opportunities, and threats.

From there, we broke down our five-year plan into yearly plans, and further divided the yearly plans by department. The yearly goals for each department were then separated into monthly departmental goals, and, finally, into monthly goals for individual employees. That process of creating broad goals and then breaking them down into tasks continues today.

The Mission Statement

It is difficult to think of any undertaking in business as that can seem as hokey and contrived as writing a mission statement. At face value, the mission of any given company usually seems fairly obvious; each business has its customers and its products or services, and the mission is simply to bring these two elements together. It seems pretty straightforward.

But at Prestwick House, drafting our formal mission statement has had a huge impact on how the company has developed. Our statement is as follows:

Prestwick House is in business for two reasons:

1) To be the premier supplier of top-quality products for English and Language Arts teachers through an aggressive program of developing innovative products focused on fulfilling teacher needs and sourcing the best products from partner companies.

2) To offer products and services to teachers at a fair profit, thereby allowing us to pursue as-yet-unknown personal, professional, and business opportunities.

With this two-part mission statement in place, we were able to take a balanced approach to developing the company. As we began to develop our first five-year plan, this statement helped us focus on our two most important goals: quality and profitability.

A mission statement is a simple, but powerful tool. When we have followed ours, we have been successful, and when we have been too proud to be bound by it, we have always fallen short of our goals.

From Mission to Action

Guided by our mission statement, we have attempted to take a balanced approach in our long-term, company-wide goals. (You can find a copy of our current strategic planning memo in the appendix section of the book.)

Each department manager takes his or her annual goals and breaks them down into monthly goals. Then, with the help of the staff, he or she will determine what role the department must play in meeting the larger company goals. This is a traditional, business-school approach, sometimes called "management by objective."

At Prestwick House, each department meets once a month to discuss progress towards these monthly goals. While meeting so often may seem excessive at first, by getting together each month in this way, we ensure that everyone is working efficiently. Rather than feeling micromanaged, workers seem to feel that they benefit from this process. Each individual's contributions are acknowledged as important, and staff members also seem to feel a great sense of accomplishment when they can report on finished projects to their managers and peers.

We believe that it is largely as a result of these frequent meetings that we are much more productive than most companies of a similar size. Knowing that a monthly meeting is only days away at any given time is like knowing that your homework is due soon. Deadlines on paper come and go, but when you have to report that you are still working on a project that is two months past its deadline, and everyone knows it—that's motivation.

Goals for "Routine" Jobs: Transactional vs. Transformational Goals

I mentioned that the process of "objectives management" is fairly traditional, but we have added our own twist to this technique with our concept of "transaction vs. transformational" goals. In each department, when we meet to discuss our monthly objectives, we take on a mixture of transactional and transformational goals.

Transactional goals will encompass the more routine functions expected of an employee. For example, many of the goals in our customer service department are transactional in that they are based on performing a rote function. So, if the stated departmental goal is to complete all the orders that come in by 3:00, then meeting that goal is important, and customer service sets out to see that those transactions are preformed at a high level.

Transactional goals make sure the job gets done. Transformational goals deal with how the job is getting done, or, more importantly, how it can be done better.

Transformational goals require that each employee has a vision of how he or she can contribute to building the company. Surprisingly, even in a department like customer service, where it would seem on the surface that all work is transactional and employees typically have little say in how the job gets done, there is always room for transformational behavior. At Prestwick House, customer service agents have the responsibility to make sure that they're improving our processes over time. For instance, if there is a day in which we do not ship all orders by 3:00, our agents ask themselves what went wrong and where there might be room for improvement. Giving employees the freedom and responsibility to improve their departments promotes creative thinking, even as it gives staff members a strong sense of ownership over their jobs and increases employee satisfaction.

Constant Communication

The Prestwick House style of strategic planning relies on communicating what is going on in the company. I have already mentioned the monthly departmental strategic-planning meetings, in which everyone reports on individual goals, but there's much more to our communication system than that. We also have a whiteboard in the company café that's updated to show our daily sales figures. Through Intraweb postings, email, and text, we make sure that everyone is aware of whether we are meeting our yearly financial goals.

One of the most important ways in which we share our progress as a company is through our quarterly meetings. Once every quarter, we pause to consider the big-picture view of how each of the various departments is progressing. Mangers from each area of the company report on their departments' achievements and may even take the time to brag a bit about staff members who have stood out during that quarter.

The Prestwick House Self-Evaluation

The last element of our communication system at Prestwick House is the annual performance review. These annual rituals are widely despised in the corporate world, and in my own experience at other companies, these meetings don't always offer a lot of value. They take up valuable time, and they often lack useful information. That's why at Prestwick House, we committed to come up with a self-evaluation process that would reflect the company's values and actually improve our customers' experience. Above all, we wanted to streamline the process.

Staff Self-Evaluation 2009

Please read and review each area and mark the box that best describes how you would rate yourself in that particular area.

1. I am very capable in my area of responsibility.

[ ] I consistently produce high quality work. I have outstanding technical knowledge of the job, and errors are very rare.

[ ] I usually produce good quality work. I have above average technical grasp of the job and make few errors.

[ ] The quality of work I produce is adequate. I have the required level of technical knowledge.

[ ] I require some coaching in this area. My technical knowledge is not yet where it should be.

Comments: _____

_____

_____

2. By achieving my goals, I have contributed to the company meeting its goals.

[ ] My goals are very clear and direct and I have made progress each month. I consistently create and achieve goals that have had a direct and immediate impact on the company. I can easily point to quantitative evidence that goals have been set and met and have had an impact.

[ ] My goals are fairly straightforward and I report on them each month. Some goals have had a direct and immediate impact on the company. I can point to quantitative evidence that some goals have been set and met and have had an impact.

[ ] I take part in the routine of goal-setting, but at times my goals do not seem to connect with company objectives. It is somewhat difficult for me to point to quantitative evidence that goals have been set and met and have had an impact.

[ ] I don't feel confident regarding my goals and wonder if they really connect with company objectives. I'd like to be able to point to quantitative evidence that goals have been set and met and have had an impact, but I'm not sure that they have.

Comments: _____

_____

_____

3. My attitude contributes to building a harmonious workplace.

[ ] I am consistently friendly and regularly extend conventional courtesies to fellow PH staff members. I consistently steer interactions towards positive solutions and away from destructive gossip, and I consistently employ cooperative, consensus-building skills to solve problems.

[ ] I am friendly and occasionally extend conventional courtesies to fellow PH staff members. I am generally adept at steering interactions towards positive solutions and away from destructive gossip, and at times I employ cooperative, consensus-building skills to solve problems.

[ ] I am friendly with and extend conventional courtesies to some PH staff members. I am not as effective at steering interactions towards positive solutions and away from destructive gossip as I probably should be. At times, I take a confrontational approach to problem solving and conflict resolution.

[ ] I don't regard myself as very friendly. I probably should be doing more to steer interactions towards positive solutions. At times, I am confrontational rather than cooperative when problems or differences arise.

Comments: _____

_____

_____

4. I volunteer to help in areas outside of my responsibility.

[ ] I am extremely cooperative and seek out opportunities to help in other areas of the company.

[ ] I am very cooperative and very willing to pitch in to help in other areas of the company.

[ ] I cooperate well and pitch in to help in other areas of the company when called upon to do so.

[ ] I pitch in to help in other areas of the company only when called upon to do so.

Comments: _____

_____

_____

5. I have demonstrated an interest in learning how to do a more efficient job.

[ ] I quickly grasp situations that need improvement and go to work filling knowledge gaps and making improvements with little hesitation.

[ ] More often than not, I independently discern areas that require improvement and go to work filling knowledge gaps and making improvements.

[ ] I make improvements and seek to fill knowledge gaps when asked.

[ ] I am in the habit of doing what is specifically instructed without much thought of becoming more efficient, and I could benefit from more coaching in this area.

Comments: _____

_____

_____

6. I am reliable.

[ ] I am consistently dependable. I am always on time. I am absent only in emergency situations. I schedule paid time off well in advance.

[ ] I am usually dependable. I am usually punctual. All absences are explained. I schedule time off in advance.

[ ] I am dependable, but frequently absent with reasonable excuses. I sometimes schedule time off on short notice.

[ ] I have had some unexplained tardiness and absences this year, and I recognize that my unscheduled and emergency time off periodically causes problems.

Comments: _____

_____

_____

At Prestwick House, we have allowed our performance appraisal system to evolve over time to reflect our core values, which has meant that we have been able to communicate clearly with our employees about what we expect of them.

Ironically, in this process, we have found that even giving negative feedback can make people feel more satisfied in their jobs. We had to learn this through trial and error, since we initially thought that being employee-friendly meant being soft in performance reviews. Fortunately, we found out quickly that employees who really want to do a good job also want to know when they are not meeting expectations. When employees gave feedback on our process, a comment we frequently saw was that reviews loaded down with positive feedback were not that helpful. Our people truly want to improve, so Prestwick House tries to keep the performance reviews tightly focused on the few key measures that we think directly impact customer satisfaction.

Prestwick House Benefits in Action

As I mentioned previously, early on, we established "being the best place to work in Delaware" as the primary "stretch" goal for our human resources operation, even before we had any official human resources staff or policies. As any worthwhile goal should, this idea has kept us alert and encouraged us to add more meaningful benefits over time. And, while we have had production and financial goals that have helped move the company forward, more than any other undertaking, the goal of being "the best place to work" in the state has created the Prestwick House we know today.

Admittedly, achieving this superlative was a pretty ludicrous goal. First of all, Prestwick House is located in Delaware—a state that is home to perennial "best place to work" champion WL Gore. On top of that, we also had to consider the expense of such an undertaking. Being the best place to work in the state sounds expensive, and at the time, the company was still little more than my father's full-time hobby.

What we quickly learned, however, was that moving towards being the best place to work didn't necessarily have to cost a lot of money. In fact, it could make us money. While there were some financial cost involved, the time and money we invested in making Prestwick House a great place to work paid off in very little time.

Early on in this process, we realized that the company we would need to focus on both tangible and intangible benefits. While employees appreciate intangible benefits like a harmonious workplace and a culture dedicated to transparency, they can't use those benefits to pay the rent. That's why we push hard to be in the top tier of pay packages for like-sized companies. We've made a practice of comparing our tangible benefits to those of other companies in our region and to the best book publishing companies in the country on a regular basis, to make sure that we are always gaining on the competition.

As a result of all these efforts, in addition to providing the typical benefits that you would expect, such as a 401(k) program, we also pay 100% of the premiums for life insurance and both long- and short-term disability insurance. Prestwick House also provides a healthcare assistance plan centered on access to a team of personal "health advocates." This program addresses a wide array of clinical and insurance issues, and coverage is free for all employees as well as their spouses, dependent children, and even parents and in-laws.

We encourage our full-time employees to pursue higher education, and to that end, we provide up to 100% tuition reimbursement for graduate and undergraduate degree programs. To date, we have fully paid for four master's degrees, and we currently have three people pursuing degrees. While that might not seem like a high number, it is important to remember that we are a company of only 30 people. That means that so far, 23% of our staff has made use of this benefit.

In addition to all these benefits, we even have an on-site gym, with locker rooms and shower facilities.

How do we keep this process of improving our benefit offerings from becoming a monster? As I mentioned earlier, our mission has two parts; in every aspect of the business, we strive for both quality and profitability. This second consideration—profitability—keeps us from being excessive in our benefits. We realize that, as nice as these other benefits may be, the best service a company can provide for its employees is to be vibrant, growing, and profitable for many years to come. Our goal of being profitable keeps us from increasing employee benefits beyond the level of sustainability.

We spend most of our adult lives at work, so the intangible benefits of working in a pleasant environment are invaluable to employees. It's important to recognize that, just as you can't use workplace harmony to pay your bills, even the most extravagant financial benefits package will quickly shrink in value if employees hate coming to work because of rampant dysfunction.

The good news is that keeping turmoil at bay in the workplace is cheap compared to health insurance. One low-cost, high-return item we provide at Prestwick House is a daily, complimentary continental breakfast of juice, fruit, and breads. We'll occasionally even set up make-your-own omelet or French toast stations.

These breakfasts are served in our central café, which is a combination meeting room and break room, with the look and feel of a coffee shop. This space and the interactions that take place there are central to our intangible benefits package. At any given time during the work day, you can find people meeting in the café to discuss current projects or just to relax.

We built the café to underscore the fact that Prestwick House is committed to having a harmonious workplace. For people who have worked in toxic or dysfunctional workplaces, being in an environment where everyone wants to maintain an emotionally healthy workplace is a real benefit.

The "Harmonious Workplace" Benefit

"Helping to contribute to building a harmonious workplace" is not the most gracefully turned phrase, but sometimes you put something down on paper, and it sticks.

This phrase has probably remained with us because it really is the center of our intangible benefits plan. Everyone at Prestwick House recognizes that fulfilling this goal is an essential part of maintaining the free and friendly atmosphere we all enjoy today.

Being a harmonious workplace does not mean everyone is happy all the time, but it does mean that we take a collective responsibility to ensure that we don't have the types of issues that other companies have with regard to negativity, politics, gossip, and general bad-vibe mongering.

We've had a great deal of success in our goal of promoting workplace harmony because our employees quickly learn from their experience here that there are a great many benefits to working in a peaceful environment. At times we've had people who, whether because of personality, upbringing, or past experiences at other workplaces, have thought that we were not serious about this goal and have gone beyond the accepted boundaries. But including "contributes to building a harmonious workplace" as an element of the performance evaluation makes it very easy to have a straightforward HR conversation about such abuses.

It is easy to bring such people into the office and ask them if they really feel that they are fulfilling their obligations to the company. We have noticed that among employees who have not had much experience in the work world, such conversations are sometimes viewed as bullying; our mandates against gossip and confrontational approaches to problem solving are perceived as detracting from their personal sovereignty or infringing on their personal identities. In such cases, people have made the choice to leave the company. They feel that Prestwick House is not a good fit for them, and in leaving, they make a choice that benefits everyone.

For people who have had experience in workplaces that don't value workplace harmony, these conversations often end differently. Such employees are usually better able to see the advantages of buying in to our workplace harmony goals and complying with our standards.

Does this system allow people to purposely cause problems for others in the company? The honest answer to that question is simply that it hasn't been a problem so far. On various occasions, we have had people who have asked us to look into situations and enforce the harmonious workplace policy. Upon investigating those situations, we have found that it is fairly easy to identify the guilty party. I suppose we could, some-day, confront a situation that would be difficult to arbitrate, but even if we should, I suspect that we would be able to sit down with both parties and tell them that they are both failing to fulfill their responsibilities.

This system works, in part, because we at Prestwick House do not think of any individual as irreplaceable. Everyone at Prestwick House is important, but no one is indispensable. It takes a team effort to maintain workplace harmony and to keep the company growing. So, while we have people who are excellent in their jobs and would be difficult to lose, we don't have anyone that we couldn't part with. In fact, having built up this culture of employee satisfaction over the years, we've found that we have always been able to upgrade when we've had to replace people who have left. We have been able to find people who value workplace harmony to replace people who do not share this goal with us.

Recruiting For Employee Satisfaction

At Prestwick House, our managers truly care about maintaining our cul-ture, and for that reason, they take organizational fit very seriously. One thing we've had to guard against, however, is allowing such consider-ations to override other, more important hiring criteria.

The most important factor to consider in the hiring process is whether a candidate is smart enough and creative enough to not only perform the job, but also to grow with the job as it evolves. Since we are an entrepreneurial company, we don't want to hire people who are not equipped to help move the company forward. Naturally, there have been times when managers have been reminded that they are not hiring someone to be a friend—they're hiring someone who will do a job for the company. Our first responsibility to the company is to hire the best person for the job. If that person is smart, we trust that he or she will recognize that helping us working towards our goals for the company's culture is part of the job.

The alternative to this practice would be to hire people for the sake of friendship and like-mindedness. Our feeling is that getting into that practice could damage the company in the long run. The company is like an ecological system, and it will thrive only if it contains different kinds of people who have complementary skill sets.

The company simply wouldn't thrive if we hired only people who were just like our General Manager, or if everyone in customer service was just like the customer-service manager. We need to hire people of different temperaments and a wide diversity of styles.

Has Prestwick House ever made mistakes and hired people who really didn't grasp what we were about? Yes. As in any hiring situation, sometimes we hire people who fit well in our system, and sometimes we don't. But, if the people we hire don't help us build the kind of company culture we need, it is important for us to correct that problem. ✿

THE BOTTOM LINE
IS THE BOTTOM LINE

CHAPTER · CHAPTER · CHAPTER · CHAPTER

8

The Employee Satisfaction
REVOLUTION

Organizational Culture

- Satisfied Customers
- Low Turnover
- High Productivity
- Recruitment Advantage
- Financial Success

Bottom Line

Employee Statisfaction

Leadership
- Strategic Planning
- Ethics
- Authentic Leadership
- Transparency

Organizational Culture
- Trust
- Communication
- Empowerment
- Fun

HR Strategies
- Work/Life Balance
- Recruitment
- Employee Motivation
- Training & Development
- Performance Appraisals

THE BOTTOM LINE
IS THE BOTTOM LINE

"...A well-substantiated relationship exists between employee engagement—the extent to which employees are committed, believe in the values of the company, feel pride in working for their employer, and are motivated to go the extra mile—and business results....This data reaffirms the remarkable ability of an engaged workforce to impact a company's bottom line."

PATRICK KULESA[1]

WHILE THE PREVIOUS CHAPTERS have been filled with suggestions for improving employee satisfaction and creating a kinder, more hospitable organization, the impact of these strategies on profitability is what matters most.

High employee satisfaction levels have a direct effect on profits. Research has found that sound management practices that positively impact employee satisfaction can improve business performance by accelerating growth and decreasing turnover. According to the Gallop organization, companies with engaged workers enjoy an EPS growth rate 26 times that of their counterparts that have lower employee-engagement levels[2].

A strong positive correlation has been documented between higher employee satisfaction and higher stock prices. Perhaps the way to happier stockholders and customers is through happier workers.

Research at Gevity describes "what a differentiator HR best practices can be in areas such as operational performance, customer satisfaction and employee turnover."[3] HR practices can significantly improve sales and profit growth, while also lowering employee turnover. And, as demonstrated by Rachel Yee, Andy Yeung, and Edwin Cheng in their study of service shops in Hong Kong, HR practices can improve not only turnover rates, but also sales and profit growth[4]. The health-care industry has recognized important links as well. HR Solutions, Inc., found similar results when they conducted an employee engagement survey at New York-Presbyterian Hospital. The hospital's president and CEO, Dr. Herbert Pardes, said the survey results "confirm that employees that put patients first are also among the most satisfied and rewarded."[5] The hospital has some impressive rankings, including #6 among America's Best Hospitals according to *US News & World Report.*[6]

A study of employees across the hospitality industry makes the case for ethical leadership affecting the bottom line. They found that "hotels whose employees believed their managers had integrity produced higher revenues than those where employees were dissatisfied with their bosses' behavior."[7]

ISR, a global consulting firm, reported findings of a 2007 survey that demonstrated "a connection between employee engagement and higher profit margins."[8]

While there are many more case studies that demonstrate the correlation between high levels of employee satisfaction and profitability, we will now shift our focus specifically to Prestwick House. After reading about their culture, leadership style, and HR strategies, you will discover the effect these practices had on their bottom line and decide for yourselves whether you want to start your own employee satisfaction revolutions.

The Prestwick House Approach
to The Bottom Line

WHEN I DISCUSSED PRESTWICK HOUSE's tangible benefits, I left out one major factor: the performance bonus. In addition to being a benefit, for me, the bonus provides rock solid proof that the employee-satisfaction approach works.

We started the bonus system in 2001, and, having shown a profit, we paid each vested employee $2,500. By 2008, we had developed the system to the point where 18% of the company's adjusted net profit went into a bonus pool. That worked out to a performance bonus of $12,500 per eligible employee in 2008.

The $12,500 figure is so surprising that it was mistakenly omitted from an article about Prestwick House that appeared in a local newspaper; the editors didn't believe that the reporter writing the story had gotten it right. In a way, I'm glad that it was left out of the article because we were not ready to contend with the number of job applications we probably would have received had that number gone public. Nevertheless, it is true that each eligible person at Prestwick House, from warehouse workers to editors and managers, received that bonus amount.

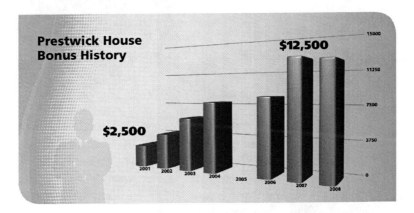

The equal distribution of the bonus pool raises some eyebrows when I mention it because some say that we are rewarding slackers along with stars. I suppose that is one way of looking at it, but not an accurate way. Under the strategic planning system, we have an ongoing process for training or weeding out underperformers. We prefer to think of the bonus as equitably rewarding the entire team for the company's success since every single job is critical to creating that success.

When setting up the bonus program, we reasoned that it would do us no good to have the best publishing department in the world if our marketing fell flat. And having a phenomenal marketing operation would be pointless if our customer-service staff failed us. Our system is predicated on the belief that every link in the chain is important, and when all the elements come together to create customer satisfaction, we all win.

And they certainly have come together for Prestwick House. We recently surveyed two separate customer pools on two separate occasions and got some startlingly good feedback on how the system is working.

When asked, "What is your general impression of Prestwick House customer service?" 76% of customers rated our customer service as "Reliable and High Quality," 16% chose "Average Quality and Dependability," and 8% selected "Other/Not Sure."

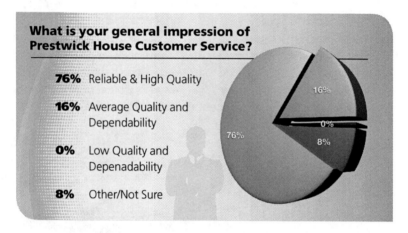

When asked to judge the statement: "Prestwick House always delivers on what they promise" a full 39% replied that the statement was "true," and 51% felt it was "very true." Just think about that for a second—90% of our customers replied that we always deliver on what we promise. I would love to patronize an airline, for example, where I could feel confident that they were always going to deliver on what they promised. Who wouldn't?

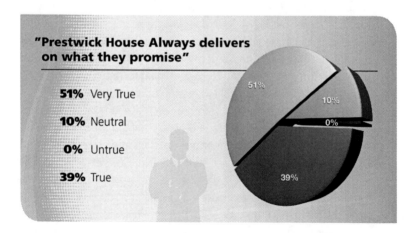

But the most revealing question was, "Would you recommend Prestwick House to a fellow teacher?" A full 98% of the survey respondents said "Yes."

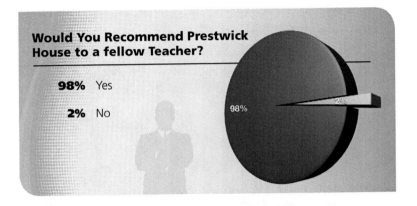

Granted, it is a survey we conducted, and the respondents represent a somewhat self-selected group, but those are staggeringly good numbers. And even now that I'm over my initial astonishment, I'm still convinced that the numbers show that the company is headed in the right direction. After all, we don't have to rely on surveys to know if we are satisfying our customers; every day they are voting on whether we stay in business with their dollars. In 2001, when we started this employee satisfaction program in earnest, our annual sales were around $2.3 million. In 2008, after eight years of consistently working to build employee satisfaction, we hit $8.3 million in sales.

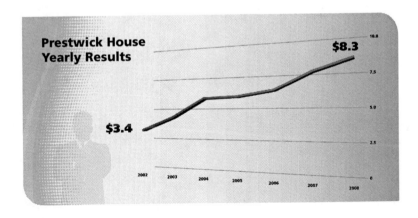

Those are not earth-shattering numbers, by big business standards, but that is a top-line sales growth rate that many companies would be eager to match.

In business, you keep score through numbers, and if our numbers show anything, they show that employee satisfaction is a real, tangible source of customer satisfaction. ✻

PARTING THOUGHTS

PARTING THOUGHTS

RESTWICK HOUSE HAS BEEN AN EXTRAORDINARY case study. The company's employee satisfaction revolution has been wildly successful in numerous ways—many of which have been quantified. This is a living organization that has clearly demonstrated the power of a satisfied staff. As you've read about Prestwick House's journey in these pages, we hope that you have been inspired to undertake a similar journey and reap your own rewards.

If you would like to share the story of your company's employee satisfaction revolution, you may email us at jason@theemployeesatisfactionrevolution.com and pat@theemployeesatisfactionrevolution.com or visit the "ES Revolution" blog at http://TheESRevolution.blogspot.com.

Every organization has the ability to leverage the potential of its employees, regardless of industry or organization size. Doing so often requires little or no cost. In fact, it's a wonder that more companies have not taken advantage of the untapped skills lying dormant in their less-than-content workers. In so doing, we add value to the business and profit to the bottom line. As Charles O'Reilly and Jeffrey Pfeffer remind us in *Hidden Value*, we can "achieve extraordinary results with ordinary people."[1] By grasping the power of fulfilled and challenged employees, we can experience some of these extraordinary results almost immediately. In putting this off, we leave exciting possibilities unexplored—now is the time to begin.

APPENDIX

OW COMMITTED IS YOUR COMPANY to employee satisfaction? Measure your company's ES IQ, or visit www.TheEmployeeSatisfactionRevolution.com for an electronic version of the test.

ESR Self-Evaluation

On a scale from 1 to 5 (with 1 meaning "strongly disagree" and 5 meaning "strongly agree"), rate your company on these employee-satisfaction measures.

1) I consider my company a great place to work.

2) My company has a clear and practical mission statement that guides management and staff in the decisions they make.

3) When establishing strategic goals, my company gets input from the people who perform the work.

4) My company encourages me to establish and work towards specific goals in my job.

5) My company allows a high degree of flexibility in how I achieve my goals.

6) My company clearly communicates company-wide strategic goals, both long and short term.

7) My company has reliable systems in place to ensure that every employee is accountable for his or her performance.

8) My company's managers provide frequent and meaningful feedback.

9) My company provides a competitive compensation package.

10) My company deals effectively with dissatisfied employees and does not allow problems to fester.

11) My company fosters an environment of fun and friendliness.

12) My company puts the need to satisfy customers above the need to satisfy policies.

13) My company's leadership lives out the values of the company.

14) Company leaders understand the value of investing in employee satisfaction.

15) When my company is successful, that success is reflected in my compensation.

Scoring:

60 or higher: Your company is an ES superstar and is probably widely regarded as a great place to work. You work for a company that understands that there is a high return on employee satisfaction, and (if publicly traded) your company probably outperforms the market.

54—59: Your company has a good start on becoming a part of the ES Revolution. You have policies and practices in place that help contribute to employee happiness, and your managers know that building employee satisfaction is a good business practice.

30—53: Your company is under-motivating and, in many ways, de-motivating employees. With so few ES practices in place, your company is less competitive than it should be, and there is a good chance that it is struggling financially as it contends with high turnover and the loss of top talent.

29 or lower: Your organization is in bad shape. It is less productive and profitable than similar types of companies that invest in ES. Your leaders are causing major morale problems by hoarding information and behaving capriciously. Many employees have probably progressed from being de-motivated to being openly hostile to the company. That hostility may be causing you to lose both employees and customers. Unless your business enjoys some sort of monopoly position in the marketplace, it is likely to struggle.

Prestwick House STrategic Planning / 2009 Goals memorandum

Corporate Goals

Total Revenue Goal: $8,652,000 (15% increase from $7,500,000 in 2008)

- We will strive for 15% increase in total revenue in 2008. This difficult, but achievable goal will focus our energy on pursuing high selling, profitable products and eliminating unproductive policies and work.

"Product Sales" Gross Margin Goal: 65%

- We will maintain a solid 65% in gross margin on product sales.

- Every department will need to develop meaningful goals for us to get $0.65 out of each $1.00 in sales. We will continue to build up our portfolio of high-margin PH materials, and we will continue to reduce errors and overstocks that erode margin over time.

Operating Profit Margin over 20%

- This is our first year incorporating a target operating profit. To accomplish this goal we will need to take cost control and efficiency seriously in every department and ensure that each department adheres to the budget disciplines needed to accomplish this goal.

Publish 20 new profitable "front list" titles.

- The publishing side of Prestwick House, with its strong gross margins, will continue to provide a safety net for our operations.

- This is the first year that we have set a target for "front list" titles in keeping with our 5 year plan to build to a 30 titles per year average volume.

In addition to these corporate level goals, we are establishing **five key corporate initiatives** for the year.

1) **4th-8th Grade Catalogue:** This new catalogue is a major initiative intended to open up new markets for Prestwick House materials. A key feature of the program is the development of a 4-6th grade vocabulary series.

2) **Courtesy Contact Program (CCP)**: This program is designed to give our customer service efforts a pro-active component while allowing individual CSR reps to track personal monthly goals that are not dependent on monthly call/order volume.

3) **Outside Sales Force Beta Testing**: Knowing that certain schools and teachers are impervious to direct mail advertising, we will begin testing the utility of an outside sales force in 2008.

4) **Expanded Paperback Discounting Program**: In order to expand our customer base by leveraging our operating efficiencies, we will begin systematically discounting top paperbacks. The program will be designed to win new customers to Prestwick House through paperback sales and then converting those customers to higher margin PH reproducible material, vocabulary, and writing

5) **IT/Web Site**:

The Bonus

If, by achieving these goals, Prestwick House is profitable, each fully vested employee will receive a bonus. The bonus pool will be set at 18% fully adjusted net profit.

With a net profit of $1,200,000, the bonus pool would be $216,000. Given 29 eligible employees, the bonus would be $7,448. Please note that this bonus figure is just a guideline. It is quite possible that our net profit could be greater or less than $1,200,000.

The bonus pool will be capped at $350,000.

"Vested employees" refers to any full-time person who is employed from January 1st 2008 to December 31st 2008. See the revised policy manual for details.

BIBLIOGRAPHY

Chapter 1

[1] Arussy, L. (2008). *Excellence Every Day: Make the Daily Choice—Inspire Your Employees and Amaze Your Customers.* Medford, New Jersey: Information Today, Inc.

[2] *U.S. Job Satisfaction Keeps Falling, The Conference Board Reports Today.* Retrieved October 1, 2009, from http://www.conference-board.org/utilities/pressdetail.cfm?press_id=2582

[3] Bardwick, J. M. (1995). *Danger in the Comfort Zone: From Boardroom to Mailroom—How to Break the Entitlement Habit That's Killing American Business.* New York: Amacom.

[4] *U.S. Job Satisfaction Keeps Falling, The Conference Board Reports Today.* Retrieved October 1, 2009, from http://www.conference-board.org/utilities/pressdetail.cfm?press_id=2582

[5] Job Satisfaction Statistics from a Harris Interactive Survey retrieved from www.careervision.org/about/pdfs/mr_jobsatisfaction.pdf

[6] Ibid.

[7] *U.S. Job Satisfaction Keeps Falling, The Conference Board Reports Today.* Retrieved October 1, 2009, from http://www.conference-board.org/utilities/pressdetail.cfm?press_id=2582

[8] Reichheld, F. F., & Teal, T. (2001). *The Loyalty Effect: The Hidden Force Behind Growth, Profits, and Lasting Value.* New York: Harvard Business School Press.

[9] Heskett, J. L., Sasser, W. E., & Schlesinger, L. A. (1997). *The Service Profit Chain.* New York City: Free Press.

[10] "Linking Employee Satisfaction with Productivity, Performance, and Customer Satisfaction," Corporate Leadership Council, July 2003.

[11] Ibid.

[12] Ibid.

[13] *Employee Engagement.* Retrieved October 1, 2009, from http://www.gallup.com/consulting/52/Employee-Engagement.aspx?version=print2008report

[14] Leimbach, Michael. (2006). "Redefining Employee Satisfaction: Business Performance, Employee Fulfillment, and Leadership Practices." Wilson Learning Worldwide, *Wilson Learning Worldwide.* Retrieved October 5, 2009, from http://wilsonlearning.com

Chapter 3

[1] Leimbach, Michael. (2006). "Redefining Employee Satisfaction: Business Performance, Employee Fulfillment, and Leadership Practices." Wilson Learning Worldwide, *Wilson Learning Worldwide.* Retrieved October 5, 2009, from http://wilsonlearning.com

[2] Heskett, J. L., Sasser, W. E., & Schlesinger, L. A. (1997). *The Service Profit Chain.* New York City: Free Press.

[3] "Linking Employee Satisfaction with Productivity, Performance, and Customer Satisfaction." Corporate Leadership Council, July 2003.

[4] Ibid.

[5] Ibid.

[6] Ibid.

[7] Ibid.

[8] Ibid.

[9] Ibid.

Chapter 4

[1] Schein, E. H. (2004). *Organizational Culture and Leadership (Jossey-Bass Business & Management)*. San Francisco: Jossey-Bass.

[2] Covey, S. M., & Merrill, R. R. (2008). *The Speed of Trust: The One Thing That Changes Everything*. New York City: Free Press.

[3] "How Do You Measure Trust?" Covey Link Worldwide, Executive Briefing, October, 2006.

[4] Arussy, L. (2008). *Excellence Every Day: Make the Daily Choice—Inspire Your Employees and Amaze Your Customers*. Medford, New Jersey: Information Today, Inc.

[5] Ibid.

[6] Christensen, J., Lundin, S. C., & Paul, H. (2000). *Fish! A Remarkable Way to Boost Morale and Improve Results*. New York: Hyperion.

[7] O'Brien, J. (2009). "*Zappos knows how to kick it.*" Retrieved October 1, 2009, from http://CNNMoney.com

[8] Ibid.

[9] Libby Sartain shares how the Yahoo! Values statement was rolled out in the video, "The People Side of Business," part of the Stanford Executive Briefings series, by Kantola Productions.

Chapter 5

[1] Leimbach, Michael. (2006). "Redefining Employee Satisfaction: Business Performance, Employee Fulfillment, and Leadership Practices." Wilson Learning *Worldwide, Wilson Learning Worldwide*. Retrieved October 5, 2009, from http://wilsonlearning.com

[2] Ibid.

[3] Jensen, Susan M., & Luthans, Fred. (2006). "Entrepreneurs as authentic leaders: impact on employees' attitudes." *Leadership and Organization Development Journal*, 27(8), 646-666.

[4] Arussy, L. (2008). *Excellence Every Day: Make the Daily Choice—Inspire Your Employees and Amaze Your Customers*. Medford, New Jersey: Information Today, Inc.

[5] Sample, S. B. (2003). *The Contrarian's Guide to Leadership (J-B Warren Bennis Series)*. San Francisco: Jossey-Bass.

[6] Goleman, D. (1995). *Emotional Intelligence: Why It Can Matter More Than IQ*. United States and Canada: Bantam.

[7] Boyatzis, R. E., Goleman, D., & Mckee, A. (2002). *Primal Leadership: Learning to Lead with Emotional Intelligence*. New York: Harvard Business School Press.

[8] Maxwell, J. C. (2006). *The 360 Degree Leader: Developing Your Influence from Anywhere in the Organization*. Waco, TX: Thomas Nelson.

[9] Arussy, L. (2008). *Excellence Every Day: Make the Daily Choice—Inspire Your Employees and Amaze Your Customers*. Medford, New Jersey: Information Today, Inc.

[10] Leeson, P. T. (2009). *The Invisible Hook: The Hidden Economics of Pirates*. Princeton: Princeton University Press.

Chapter 6

[1] "Gevity-Cornell University Study: Retailers Experience Nearly 75 Percent Less Turnover through Defined Work Strategies: Surveys of 243

Small Businesses also Show Improved Customer Satisfaction, Employee Commitment among Professional Services, Manufacturing Industries." (2007, June 27). Staff Prime Zone Media Network.

[2] Edmans, Alex. (2008). "How Investing in Intangibles—Like Employee Satisfaction—Translates into Financial Returns." *Knowledge@Wharton*. Retrieved October 5, 2009, from http://knowledge.wharton.upenn

[3] Ibid.

[4] "Gevity-Cornell University Study: Retailers Experience Nearly 75 percent Less Turnover through Defined Work Strategies: Surveys of 243 Small Businesses also Show Improved Customer Satisfaction, Employee Commitment among Professional Services, Manufacturing Industries." (2007, June 27). Staff Prime Zone Media Network

[5] Ibid.

[6] Job Satisfaction Survey. (2009). Public Policy Polling. Rleith, NC.

[7] Henderson, David and Sandy Wayne. (2007). "Not All Responses to Breach are the Same: The Interconnection of Social Exchange and Psychological Contract Processes in Organizations." *Academy of Management Journal.*

[8] Pillsbury, Dennis H. (2007). "Everybody Have Fun Tonight," Rough Notes, v. 150, I 12, p 18 (5).

Chapter 7

[1] "Employee Engagement: What's Your Engagement Ratio?" Gallop Consulting, Washington, DC, 2008

[2] Edmans, Alex. (2008). "How Investing in Intangibles—Like Employee Satisfaction—Translates into Financial Returns." *Knowledge@Wharton*. Retrieved October 5, 2009, from http://knowledge.wharton.upenn

[3] Ibid.

[4] Collins, C., Ericksen, J., and Allen, M. (2005). *Research report on Phase 3 of the Cornell University/Gevity Institute Study – Employee outcomes: Human resource management practices and firm performance in small businesses*

(CAHRS Working Paper #08-09). Ithaca, NY: Cornell University, School of Industrial and Labor Relations, Center for Advanced Human Resource Studies. http://digitalcommons.ilr.cornell.edu/cahrswp/486

[5] Yee, Rachel W.Y., Andy C.L. Yeung, and T.C. Edwin Cheng (2008). "The impact of employee satisfaction on quality and profitability in high-contact service industries." *Journal of Operations Management.* v 26 I 5 p 651 (18).

[6] "New York-Presbyterian Tops List for Employee satisfaction and Concern for Patient Care among Academic Medical Centers: Survey Shows Hospital Judged Best of Class in Attention to Patient Care, Communication, and Job Satisfaction." (2008, December 29). http://nyp.org/news/hospital/employee-satisfaction-concern.html

[7] Ibid.

[8] Berta, Dina. (2008). "Study: managers' integrity integral to employee satis-faction" Nation's Restaurant News. Nov 17, 2008 v 42 i45 p 12(1).

[9] Spors, K. *Why Employee Satisfaction Bolsters Profitability*—Independent Street—WSJ. Retrieved October 6, 2009, from http://blogs.wsj.com/indepen-dentstreet/2008/09/22/why-employee-satisfaction-bolsters-profitability/

Chapter 8

[1] "Engaged employees help boost the bottom line" (2006) HR.com

[2] "Employee Engagement: What's Your Engagement Ratio?" (2008). Gallop Consulting, Washington, DC.

[3] Collins, Christopher, Jeff Ericksen, and Matthew Allen. (2005). *Research report on Phase 3 of the Cornell University/Gevity Institute Study – Employee outcomes: Human resource management practices and firm performance in small businesses* (CAHRS Working Paper #08-09). Ithaca, NY: Cornell University, School of Industrial and Labor Relations, Center for Advanced Human Resource Studies. http://digitalcommons.ilr.cornell.edu/cahrswp/486

[4] Yee, Rachel W.Y., Andy C.L. Yeung, and T.C. Edwin Cheng. (2008). "The impact of employee satisfaction on quality and profitability in high-contact service industries." *Journal of Operations Management.* v 26 I 5 p 651 (18).

[5] *NewYork-Presbyterian Tops List for Employee Satisfaction and Concern for Patient Care Among Academic Medical Centers - New York Presbyterian Hospital.* Retrieved October 6, 2009, from http://nyp.org/news/hospital/employee-satisfaction-concern.html

[6] Ibid.

[7] Berta, Dina. (2008). "Study: managers' integrity integral to employee satisfaction." *Nation's Restaurant News.* Nov 17, 2008 v 42 i45 p 12(1).

[8] Spors, K. *Why Employee Satisfaction Bolsters Profitability—Independent Street—WSJ.* Retrieved October 6, 2009, from http://blogs.wsj.com/independentstreet/2008/09/22/why-employee-satisfaction-bolsters-profitability/

Chapter 9

[1] O'Reilly, C. A. (2000). *Hidden Value: How Great Companies Achieve Extraordinary Results with Ordinary People.* New York: Harvard Business School Press.